PSYCHOLOGY
An Outline for the Intending Student

CONTRIBUTORS

John Cohen

Neville Moray

Andrew H. Gregory

Richard Skemp

R. C. Oldfield

Gustav Jahoda

PSYCHOLOGY

An Outline for the Intending Student

Edited by

Professor John Cohen
Department of Psychology
University of Manchester

LONDON
ROUTLEDGE & KEGAN PAUL

First published 1968
by Routledge & Kegan Paul Ltd
Broadway House, 68–74 Carter Lane
London, E.C.4

Printed in Great Britain
by Richard Clay (The Chaucer Press), Ltd
Bungay, Suffolk

SBN 7100 2998 5 (P)
SBN 7100 6027 0 (C)

CONTENTS

CONTENTS

vi

FIGURES

6   SOCIAL BEHAVIOUR

PREFACE

OUR PRIMARY AIM in writing this book is to introduce the subject of Psychology to pupils in the upper forms of Grammar Schools who might be interested in taking it up at a university or in becoming familiar with its problems, methods and goals as part of what has come to be called General Studies.

It would have been out of the question to attempt to cover the entire field of psychological science in a brief introduction. We have therefore limited ourselves to sampling and sketching a few of the main topics generally agreed to belong to the heart of the subject. We hope that the result of our efforts will also be of value to students in Colleges of Education and Colleges of Further Education.

Psychology can now be studied at most British universities thanks to a remarkable expansion of facilities in recent years. The great diversity in the way the degree courses are organised, and their relations with degree courses in allied disciplines has now, however, become very baffling to the intending student. We have accordingly prepared an Appendix which we hope will help the candidate to find his way through the bewildering maze of different entry requirements.

JOHN COHEN

ACKNOWLEDGEMENTS

I SHOULD LIKE TO THANK my fellow authors for their helpfulness and patience in preparing their respective chapters with our common aim in mind. My thanks are also due to Mr. Brent Skelly, a former Research Assistant, who helped in the compilation of the Appendix in its early stages, and to all Heads of Departments of Psychology in the universities of Great Britain who co-operated in providing and checking the details relating to their Departments. Here, too, I should include Dr. Timothy Shallice of University College, London, and Mr. James Reason of the University of Leicester. In some instances, as in the case of St. Andrews and Dundee, the complexity of the administrative situation led to a considerable and time consuming correspondence.

Thanks are also due to the following for permission to reproduce graphs and diagrams in this volume:

The American Psychological Association for material originally appearing in the *Journal of Experimental Psychology*; The British Psychological Society for material originally appearing in the *British Journal of Psychology;* William Heffer Ltd. for material originally appearing in the *Quarterly Journal of Experimental Psychology*; the Editor of *Nature*; Penguin Books Ltd.; John Wiley and Sons Inc., New York.

J.C.

I

Psychology As Science

John Cohen

What Psychology Is About

Psychology is not a school subject, yet. The result is that many pupils have vague or even bizarre notions of what it is all about, whether as taught at universities or as practised, say, by occupational psychologists in industry or by clinical psychologists in the National Health Service. Unless a schoolboy has a friend who is already a university student of psychology, or knows a professional psychologist, he is apt to rely for his information on somewhat dubious sources, on out-of-date or misleading books which he discovers on the shelves of local libraries, on an occasional broadcast, television programme, film, newspaper article or on old wives' tales. I have met sixth-formers who believe that psychology is the royal road to self-knowledge or that it gives secret access to the thoughts of others. Some imagine that students of psychology learn, first of all, how to practise hypnosis, how to interpret dreams or how to engage in telepathy or clairvoyance. Not a few think of the psychologist as someone who can test, with unerring accuracy, all human talents and aptitudes and measure all human virtues and vices. These views are wide of the mark.

Psychology is often spoken of as the science of mind and behaviour. Rather than take this as a hard and fast definition, which could be hotly disputed, let us rather consider what the subject is about. This is perhaps less arguable. It is about people (and animals). How do we make sense of the world of colours, shapes and sounds, of persons and things around us? How do we grow up mentally and

1

emotionally to become what we are? What, in fact, is mental growth? How do we learn to speak and acquire the manual, social and other skills that we employ during the course of our lives? How (and why) do we remember and forget? What makes us choose this or that, or decide this or that? What makes us feel fatigued or under stress? What goes on in us when we love or hate? What happens to us when we fall asleep and dream? These are typical questions that occupy the psychologist as *investigator*. Psychology, as science, may thus be said to explore the manner in which we think and behave, the conditions under which we do so, and the why and wherefore of all this.

Professional psychologists, who are engaged in the practical application of their subject, have a variety of tasks. Sometimes they try to discover what ails an individual or group and to propose, or put into effect, remedial action. This work goes on, for example, in Child Guidance Clinics and in centres for dealing with backward, retarded, emotionally disturbed or handicapped children. Often the psychologists act as advisers to their employers in industry and commerce, or in the armed forces, or to those who administer mental or other hospitals, occupational rehabilitation centres, prisons or other social institutions. In the field of mental health they generally work closely with psychiatrists. Sometimes they themselves are executives and not simply advisers. They are, that is, empowered to take action with respect to particular persons or situations; guiding individuals in the choice of a career by assessing their abilities, aptitudes and inclinations; determining the best form of training for different tasks; assisting in the rehabilitation of those disabled by birth or misfortune; or in organising market research or schemes of advertising.

Because of its links with many sciences, pure and applied, as well as with the arts, psychology cannot stand, so to speak, alone. The human 'mind' does not exist in a disembodied vacuum any more than the individual person exists in a social or historical vacuum. The student of psychology therefore needs to be trained in other disciplines as well. He has, fortunately, a wide range of choice depending on his interests and capacities. Some familiarity with biology, mathematics and physics is more or less essential for every student of psychology. The kind of advanced training he needs will, however, vary with the particular field in which he wishes to specialise or become a practitioner. For instance, if he intends to work in what is called 'operational research', or in some way connected with computer science or cybernetics, he will have to take a stiffer dose of mathematics, physics and electronics. He will need to be well grounded in neurophysiology if he hopes to work with clinical neurologists engaged in treating brain-injured patients, and he will need a broad training in pharmacology and related sciences if he intends to become a psychopharmacologist occupied in the study of the effects of drugs on man, a subject of rapidly growing interest. By contrast, a knowledge of sociology and social anthropology is certainly helpful for work in industrial management or market research. There is an old saying 'Who is wise? He who learns from all men.' This is particularly apt for the psychologist, who should always be prepared to learn from all people at all times and in all places. Everything is grist for the psychological mill. No source of knowledge should be despised, no common observation scorned or brushed aside, nothing dismissed as 'familiar'. More than anyone else the psychologist stands to gain from open-mindedness and to lose from a narrowness of vision or interest.

In Britain the majority of psychologists are in favour of professionalism in their subject. Moreover, the British Psychological Society approves of professional practitioners in psychology, provided they are properly qualified. The Society grades those who belong to it as plain members, Associates or Fellows. Nevertheless, a minority of psychologists have expressed misgivings about the scientific basis of professionalism in their discipline. They do not like to see application or practice run ahead of adequately established theory. In Britain, anyone has the right at present to call himself a 'psychologist' if he is so inclined, and to put up a plaque publicising his claims. There is nothing in law to prevent this. In some countries (e.g. Holland) measures are to be taken to secure legal protection for the title 'psychologist' so that it may only be used by those with approved training, as in medicine and dentistry. However, even if this measure were to be adopted in Britain it would not satisfy the critics, for their doubts are not so much based on the dangers of charlatanism and quackery but on their view that psychological science has not yet reached the stage at which it could provide a clear and reliable basis for use in actual social situations, for instance, in the spheres of industry, education or health.

It is rare to find a sixth-former with a clear understanding of the difference between psychology and psychiatry. Let us therefore face the distinction between them. Psychiatry is part of medicine. Psychiatrists are medically trained and are largely occupied with the diagnosis and treatment of mental and emotional disorder. What is commonly called 'social psychiatry' deals especially with the social and occupational readjustment of mental patients. There are a few hospitals for social psychiatry in which there is little individual treatment as such, the care of the patient taking the form of arranging participation for him in various forms of group life. Social psychiatry is thus akin to the theory and practice of social psychology. Preventive psychiatry, that is, the study of measures to prevent mental disorder, is still in its infancy. A major difficulty is that, unlike many forms of physical illness, mental illness involves more than the patient himself, for its essential feature is the disruption of his relations with other people and with society as a whole.

The relation between psychology and psychiatry is rather like that between physiology, which is the study of the normal functioning of the body, and pathology, which is the study of the diseased body. But the analogy is not complete, for the relation between psychology and psychiatry is more complex than that between physiology and pathology. Psychiatry, unlike pathology, is not a 'pure' science, since its main task is treatment. Furthermore, as hinted above, psychiatrists often work in collaboration with clinical psychologists in the diagnosis of mental illness, in evaluating the effectiveness of therapy, and in the rehabilitation of the patient.

Psychoanalysis, again, is not the same as psychiatry, although some psychiatrists use the methods of psychoanalysis in their dealings with patients. The word 'psychoanalysis' itself is ambiguous for it may refer to (i) a body of theory and practice deriving from the discoveries of Sigmund Freud; (ii) the free-association and other techniques that Freud devised for the examination and treatment of patients suffering from mental and emotional difficulties; or (iii) the *treatment itself* which is based on the theory and techniques.

Psychoanalysis is accordingly associated with the name of Freud, and institutes of psychoanalysis in Britain as elsewhere, follow Freudian principles and teaching. In order to become an accredited psychoanalyst the practitioner need not be, though he usually is, medically qualified, but he has to undergo a prescribed training, including psychoanalysis, over a specified period.

Psychoanalysis is often regarded as part of psychology in the broad sense. Indeed, many of the ideas employed by psychoanalysts are much the same as those found in academic psychology, but this is obscured by the use of different terminologies, not to speak of the jargon that finds its way into psychological textbooks. A good case could be made for showing that very many expressions in psychoanalysis have essentially the same meaning as corresponding words used by those who prefer to speak in terms of what is supposed to go on in the nervous system rather than in terms of what is supposed to go on in the so-called 'unconscious' part of the mind. Examples of these expressions are *regression* (a return to less 'mature' forms of behaviour); *fixation* (an excessive attachment to someone or something which is formed in infancy and persists for long afterwards in inappropriate fashion); *ambivalence* (the tendency to be pulled in psychologically opposite directions, e.g. loving and hating the same person); *repression* (keeping things out of one's consciousness without realising it). Nevertheless, there can be no question that the work of Freud and his followers has shed a flood of light on aspects of human life which were previously ill-understood. It has also had a profound effect on the interpretation and appreciation of art, on literature, literary criticism and biography, on the study of comparative religion and on many other important elements of human culture.

I have so far referred only to the Freudian school of psychoanalysis. There are other schools, notably the Jungians, followers of the late C. G. Jung, who had much to say on the 'collective' as distinct from the personal unconscious. There are also the existentialists, who engage in a subtle analysis of the patient's actual situation and circumstances.

However, the majority of scientific psychologists, not entirely without justification, feel a little estranged from the speculative and 'cultish' features of these groups. The analysts, with equal justice, could hit back at the self-styled 'scientific' psychologists and accuse them of dogmatism, doctrinaire methods and an impoverished notion of human behaviour.

The future student of psychology should therefore not be surprised to find that the examination of intimate personal experience is not given much space in the academic textbooks. If this is what chiefly interests him he will have to turn to writers on psychoanalysis and psychotherapy. The reason for the omission is that academic psychologists prefer to devote themselves to those parts of the subject which can be treated with some degree of precision. The complexities of the inner life are hard to investigate with any rigour. One cannot perform a laboratory experiment on 'falling in love'. One cannot measure hate, ambition, jealousy as one can, say, the capacity of the eye to see in the dark. Hence many psychologists have retreated from the study of subjective experience. So much so, that any remark a person makes about his own state of mind is often regarded as unverifiable and therefore denied a place in psychological science.

This trend on the whole has been a good thing in so far as it has emphasised the need for objectivity in contrast to mere personal opinion. But it has gone too far and the pendulum now seems to be swinging the other way. Compare statements such as 'I am worried' or 'I hate you' with statements such as 'I am hot' or 'my hand is trembling'. The latter are verifiable in a way which is not possible for the former. Yet if we limited psychology to the second sort of statement, we should not be able to speak of kindness, greed, remorse or hope. Nor, strictly speaking, could we speak of colours, of the loudness or pitch of sounds, or of the fragrance of flowers. The experience of pain is particularly instructive. A doctor can measure my temperature and say whether I am too hot or too cold (as judged by average temperature), but he cannot assert that I am in pain if I deny it nor can he deny it if I assert it. If psychology is to deal with human experience, it must not impose upon itself a demand for an impossible kind of objectivity.

Classification of Psychological Information

The vast field of study called 'psychology' can be subdivided in numerous ways, of which the following are examples:

(i) by the age group studied (the psychology of childhood, adolescence, etc.);

(ii) by the normality of the group (the psychology of the insane, the brain injured, etc.);

(iii) by field of application (educational, occupational, etc.);

(iv) by the process studied (perceiving, learning, thinking, etc.).

There is a sense in which it is correct to say that all psychology is social, for man is, biologically speaking, a social animal. Everyone comes into life blessed or burdened with an incalculably long ancestral past. Everyone is born into a family group, and participates in a number of others. The very words we utter are essentially social. The culture of the society in which we live, and the traditions which we inherit are social influences. What is commonly called social psychology is that part of psychology chiefly concerned with group processes and effects as such, rather than with what goes on, so to speak, within individuals. Social psychology is more concerned with the team than with the separate players.

One way of showing how the study of psychology is organised is by the system of classification used in a journal called *Psychological Abstracts*. This provides a brief summary of psychological articles and books published all over the world, and it employs the following classificatory scheme:

I. General
II. Methodology and Research Technology
III. Experimental
IV. Physiological
V. Animal
VI. Developmental
VII. Social
VIII. Personality
IX. Clinical
X. Educational
XI. Military and Personnel

This scheme is only one of many possible ones, and might be criticised on various grounds. It could be pointed out, for instance, that animal, developmental and clinical psychology have in common a considerable social element. And it is open to the logical objection that the basis of classification is not uniform. Thus II and III have to do with methods, but IV (which overlaps with V) has to do with the body–mind contrast, and V is a species group. VI, again, is an age group. The scheme is defective, but as a rough, working guide to the activities of psychologists, it has its advantages.

In a brief, introductory book such as the present, the aim of which is to provide information about the scope and substance of psychological science, there is only room for selected topics. I have chosen those which at the same time are central to the subject, attract wide interest and are actively investigated. It seems possible to cover much of present-day psychology under our six chapter headings, which embrace items I to VII in the *Psychological Abstracts*.

8

Mind and Brain

Strange as it may seem, the fact that what we call mind is linked with brain in the most intimate way is a comparatively modern discovery, so far as any detailed understanding of this link is concerned. If we may judge from the rock carvings found near the west coast of Sweden, and dating back to the Bronze Age, about 1000 B.C., it seems that little importance was at that time attached to the brain. The carvings represent human figures with relatively tiny heads and very long and powerful arms and legs, as if what was inside the head had little to do with behaviour.

The earliest reference to the contents of the human skull is found in the papyri of ancient Egypt. When the Egyptians embalmed their dead, they first got rid of the brain, which they treated as waste matter, for they believed that the soul or spirit resides in the heart, and the power of judgement in the kidneys. At the embalming, an incision was made in the left flank of the corpse for the removal of the lungs and abdominal organs, which were preserved in canopic jars or, at a later period, replaced in the body. According to the Greek historian Herodotus, the Egyptians scooped out part of the brain through the left nostril and disposed of the rest of it by rinsing the skull with a corrosive liquid.

The Babylonians, on the other hand, believed that the liver, not the heart, was the seat of the emotions and passions. They attributed each different feeling to some activity in a particular part of the liver. Their seers and prophets were all expert at reading livers with the aim of detecting signs of future events, much as a superstitious person today might read leaves in a teacup, and they trained their young men for future careers as liver readers by the use of clay and stone models of the liver in the same sort of way as a modern medical student studies a model of the brain.

In ancient India, China and Tibet, no notice was taken of the brain, and the body as a whole was thought of as a miniature universe. The soul, which was supposed to 'pop' in at birth was believed to spread out through the body by means of a large number of ducts.

Alcmaeon of Croton (fifth century B.C.), a disciple of Pythagoras, seems to have been the first to recognise the fundamental association between brain and mind. His belief was shared by some other early Greek philosophers, but not by one of the most celebrated of them, Aristotle, who, like Homer and the Egyptians, regarded the heart as the seat of mind. Aristotle's teacher, Plato, conceived of the mind or soul on a tripartite basis, its three components, vegetative, vital and rational, corresponding to the essential nature of plant, animal and man respectively. The vegetative soul, serving the appetites, was located in the pelvis and belly; the vital soul, which generated bodily heat, was placed in the chest, while the rational faculties found a suitable resting-place in the head. It has been suggested that Plato was led to this threefold subdivision of the mind by reflecting on the three main social groups in the Athens of his day: the workers (vegetative), the military (vital) and the intellectual elite (rational).

Nowadays, nearly all psychologists, regardless of the school of thought to which they belong, recognise the close relation between mental experience and brain. Everyone acknowledges, therefore, the value for psychology of neurophysiological and electrochemical methods of studying the brain. Such methods will ultimately help to unravel the complexities of mental disturbance which results from damage to particular parts of the brain, such as *aphasia* or impairment of the ability to use language, *agnosia* or loss of the ability to interpret sense impressions or to recognise familiar objects, and *apraxia* or impairment of the ability to perform a sensible sequence of movements. The task of the physiological psychologist is to identify the causes of such disturbances, to trace the patterns of mental deterioration which are connected with different injuries or lesions, and to employ experimental techniques in rehabilitating the patients.

The link between mind and brain is dramatically observed in the effect on consciousness of any injury to the brain or even of a blow on the head. This effect enables us to clarify the notion of consciousness. We are all familiar with the words 'conscious' and 'consciousness' although these cannot be strictly defined except in terms of themselves. How could we describe consciousness to someone who had never been conscious? Common usage of the word 'conscious' assumes it to refer to something that varies in degree, ranging from full consciousness through a state of clouding of consciousness, to an unconscious state. Apart from such degrees in *clarity*, there are also degrees in the extent to which the *content* of consciousness is intact. Thus, under a local anaesthetic we say that there is a loss of consciousness for a particular part of the body which is now insensitive. Yet a man may be totally paralysed while retaining his full consciousness. This shows that consciousness does not depend on the ability to move our limbs as we please. We can say, then, that consciousness varies in at least two dimensions, namely, clarity and content.

Furthermore, it is convenient to consider consciousness as relating only to part of our experience. By 'experience' we mean all the 'information' about the external world which the brain receives through the sense organs and 'converts' into something we describe as mental. The manner whereby this 'conversion' takes place remains a mystery. We also include under 'experience' the mental outcome of the spontaneous activity of the brain. Only a fraction of all this information enters awareness at any given time, and some of it may never enter awareness. We have to suppose that a complex system of filters governs the relation between experience and consciousness, that is to say, regulates that part of our experience of which we become aware.

Finally, there is the question of defining consciousness in such a way as to make sense in every context of human experience. A contemporary psychologist proposes that consciousness should mean one thing for the scientist and another for the theologian. This view is at least arguable. No physiologist insists that cardiac function should be defined in different ways for the scientist and theologian respectively. If the theologian has any valid observations to make on the nature of consciousness, the psychologist is bound to reckon with them in a scientific definition. If, on the other hand, the theologian has nothing valid to contribute, the psychologist can safely disregard him.

Explanation in Psychology

The idea that psychology is a collection of interesting facts about human nature embodies only a partial truth. Like other sciences, psychology is not only concerned with discovering and describing facts but also with explaining them. This presupposes a theory or model which puts the facts into perspective. Properly speaking, the word 'psychology' should perhaps refer to such theoretical perspectives, however provisional they may be, rather than to assemblies of factual information. On this view, the task of psychology is primarily to systematise the facts, to give them order and meaning, thus enabling us to understand, and possibly to predict, human behaviour.

The question of explanation crops up again and again in all parts of psychology. It is, indeed, the basic issue. But we must take care not to oversimplify. For many differences in viewpoint which the student will meet often stem from disagreement over the question: what, in fact, constitutes explanation in psychology? When, in other words, can we say that something is psychologically explained?

Unfortunately, there is no generally agreed answer to this question. So the explanations and theories which are offered may depend on the personality, temperament or personal taste of the theorist, or on the particular kind of training he has received, rather than on logic or reason or on a completely dispassionate appraisal of the facts.

The ordinary person thinks of psychological explanation as an answer to the question 'What makes a man tick?' The form of this question itself assumes a model, namely, that a man is like a watch and the psychologist is someone who opens it and looks into the mechanism. For the ordinary person, therefore, psychology seems to peer into a man's brain or mind with a sort of mental magnifying glass, in the way a watchmaker inspects the watch he is repairing.

There may well be an error here which is shared by a number of psychological theories. This is their tacit assumption that the clue to human behaviour lies somehow hidden in the secret crevices of the skull. If you dissect the brain or mind into ultimate 'elements', the mystery will be solved.

The view that all explanations in psychology must be expressed in terms of what is supposed to be happening in the nervous system leads to the expectation that a sufficiently detailed scrutiny of nerve processes will eventually yield the answers to all our questions about mind. This may or may not be true. Perhaps we can draw an analogy between physics and psychology. There was a time when physicists believed that if they could penetrate the interior of the atom, they could solve the problem of the nature of matter. In the result many riddles remain in spite of the depth of the probe, and new problems have come to light.

In psychology too, the mystery of mind will not necessarily grow less the more microscopic the analysis of the cellular and nervous structure of the brain. It would be nice if it were true that the clues were hidden *somewhere*, if only one knew where. Unfortunately, things are not so simple. Einstein remarked in his autobiography that we may have to try to understand nature rather in the manner of a watchmaker who has to study a watch without ever being able to open it. If this observation is true of psychology, the hope of unravelling the complexities of mind by penetrating deeper into the micro-structure of the brain may be a vain one. For all our analyses of the brain, however refined, would be no more, in principle, than the readings of the watchmaker while observing the dial of his watch.

This view does not conflict with what was said in the previous section about the dependence of mind on brain and the intimate relation between them. The apparent inconsistency is removed if we acknowledge at least two different levels on which psychological investigation may proceed. At one level, as illustrated in the earlier section, we can regard the psychological process as wholly dependent on the state of the brain. Much of what we include under perception, learning and remembering, and much of what governs

speech and its disturbances, are entirely governed by the
brain (see Chapters 2 and 3). Furthermore, normal functioning and development of the brain is vital if certain kinds
of serious behaviour disorders are to be avoided. The frequency with which disturbed behaviour follows an attack of
epidemic encephalitis in childhood is evidence of this. Moreover, abnormal behaviour results directly from hormone
imbalance. At this level, therefore, neurophysiological explanation may be adequate.

At the level, however, which relates to what we sometimes call the higher mental processes, we are less satisfied
by such an explanation. We would not be content to say,
for example, that honesty or dishonesty, bravery or coward-
ice, generosity or meanness merely reflect peculiarities of the
brain, or that some people prefer the Labour party to the
Conservative party, or vice versa, merely because of different
properties of their respective brains. An encyclopaedic
knowledge of Shakespeare's brain might enable us to understand how it was that he was able to write *Hamlet*, but it
would not tell us why he wanted to write it, what he felt
like while writing it, or what we feel like when reading it,
or why we value it as a great human achievement.

Different theoretical approaches in psychology all try to
set up a model for the study of human behaviour. This
process of setting up a model, or 'modelling' for short, may
be among the most fundamental of human activities. All
similes and metaphors are forms of model. We understand
a thing better if we compare it or identify it with something
else. When a child calls a twinkling star a 'blinking eye', or
the dewdrops on the grass 'tears', he is using eyes and tears
as models for stars and dew. This is a source of delight for
the child, which must be akin to the poet's joy when he hits
upon a striking metaphor. Much of a child's play is an
acting out of the assumption that his model is true, that, for
example, the crust of bread that he has bitten into is an
elephant and that his open match-box is a garage in which
he can park his tiny cars.

There is also a modelling which takes place on an
emotional plane and which has a certain formal resemblance

to intellectual modelling. A child models himself on his parents, a pupil on his teacher or on his comic strip hero. From Hercules to Batman all peoples have had their models. In this sense, the need for models enters into all intellectual, emotional and social development.

There are allied senses in which the word model can be used. We speak of a model child, a fashion model, an artist's model. Basically, the word model refers to a relatively simple representation of a complex state of affairs. In science this can amount to a representation of a set of ideas in words, in graphical form, in a mechanism, or a mathematical function. While the model is simpler that that which is being represented it nevertheless embodies the essential features. It is unusual, to say the least, for a model to be less simple than that which it represents.

If we go back far enough in history, before the development of modern science, we shall come across models in psychology and neurology based on analogies drawn from contemporary technology. Thus Galen, a physician who lived in the second century, based his conception of the brain and nervous system on the hydraulic system familiar to him from everyday life, in reservoirs, aqueducts, fountains, baths and sewers. In this respect he resembled the great French thinker Descartes, who, fifteen hundred years later, conceived of the nerves as hollow tubes rather like the bell ropes of his time which were used to summon attendants.

The hydraulic model of Galen in the second century A.D. is perhaps the most ancient of models employed to represent the human brain and mind, although Homer long before him spoke of the 'liquid soul', and this metaphor found its way into the writings of later Greek philosophers. It appealed to Descartes who wrote that the spirit or soul of man 'determines the course of that very subtle liquid which is called the animal spirits, which, running continually from the heart by the brain into the muscles, is the cause of all the movements of our limbs'. It also found a place in biology, and suggested to Galvani the flow of electric current. Freud, too, in his notion of libido or flow of energy, returns to the same model.

15

The most common type of model found in the literature of psychology is based, by analogy, on another subject which has been more fully explored. Indeed, the choice of models in psychology has been influenced by the dominant or fashionable science of the time. Thus, as from the seventeenth to the twentieth century, physics, chemistry, zoology and geology, achieved the prestige of established disciplines, psychological theorists looked to them in turn for inspiration. More recently models in psychology have leaned on developments in cybernetics (or the theory of communication and control in man and machine). We have, for instance, the gravitational analogy of Thomas Hobbes (1588–1679) who wrote that 'everyone is compelled to seek what is good for him and to avoid what is bad for him by a necessity not less than that which compels the stone to fall downward'. John Stuart Mill in the nineteenth century suggested an analogy between psychological and chemical processes, the supposed coalescence of ideas being said to resemble the process of chemical fusion. Others, influenced by geology, were attracted by the notion that the mind takes shape during the developmental years in the form of strata, each new stratum being superimposed on an existing one, rather like a succession of geological formations; and that the procedure of mental testing resembles the sinking of shafts into the mind at critical points in a manner reminiscent of the oil prospector.

A contemporary psychologist, Jean Piaget, has drawn from zoology the idea of what he has called 'a sort of embryology of intelligence'. The system that he has developed might be properly described as embryological psychology in that it tries to identify structures (of a mental kind) and trace their maturation and growth.

The growing interest in cybernetics in recent decades has led to the popularity of cybernetic models in psychology. These display self-regulating and adaptive features coupled with the properties of a communication system which receives, processes and transmits information by means of coding devices.

Computer science is yet another source of inspiration for psychologists. The investigator writes a programme for analysis by the computer about the behaviour he is studying. With the aid of the computer he can generate predictions from his model, these predictions then being checked against observation.

Few of these models or analogies are intended to imply an identity between a psychological and some other system. They are rather of the 'as if' type. For example, let us suppose that we judge the time (without consulting a watch) *as if* we had a sort of mental clock inside our brains. We can then try to specify the properties of such a 'fictitious' internal clock if it is to do the job of enabling us to judge the time, with more or less accuracy, and with the distortions that come with mood, fatigue and other factors.

This is as it should be, for much of the value of an analogy in science stems from the imperfection of the assumed resemblance. If the model were an exact replica of the original it would be no more useful than the original in prompting further questions for research except in so far as its smaller size might render it more manageable. A small model locomotive may be a precise miniature of the original. It is an exact copy in the sense that all the parts are in their proper proportions but the full power supply is lacking. Such models resemble toys, though a good toy can act as intellectual stimulus. On the other hand, if there is too little resemblance between a model and the original, or if the resemblance is far-fetched, it may mislead more than it helps.

Some theorists prefer models of another sort, not the 'as if' type but those that have a one-to-one correspondence with the original. They may prefer to use a neurophysiological model in the belief that all statements in psychology must be compatible with neurophysiology. There are some who go further and imagine that neurophysiology will eventually make a 'take-over bid', so to speak, to absorb the whole of psychology. Yet interpretations in neurophysiology must make sense in the light of psychological principles, on the grounds that psychology is the more basic of the two subjects.

There is one thing that can be said about explanation in pychology that all scientific investigators would probably accept. That is, the model or theory must be testable, by

17

some means or other. The model maker is obliged to allow other workers to make predictions from his model which can be checked by them. If the predicted observations tally with the model, so far so good. Otherwise, the model has to be revised.

This, at least, rules out useless theories, or metaphysical speculations which do not lead to scientific advance. Metaphysical speculation about life and death, the existence of God, the origin of the universe, the destiny of man and the ultimate nature of good and evil has a place of honour in human culture, but it is outside the scope of psychology. The need to be able to test a theory also rules out theories that count on their sheer bewildering effect. As Sir Cyril Burt has said, 'the pseudo scientist believes that the hall-mark of a perfect scientific theory is that it shall be so constructed as to baffle any attempts to negatise it'. On the contrary, the easier it is to refute a theory, the more useful it is, other things being equal.

But the criterion of testability does not guarantee an *inspiring* theory. For this, one needs not only a profound understanding of the subject-matter, but also imagination, a vague but nevertheless very important word.

Psychology as Art

In the foregoing pages I have written about psychology as a science. There is, however, a sense in which we could speak of psychology as belonging to the arts. Or perhaps, better still, as a bridge between the arts and sciences. This feature of psychology marks it from other sciences and has prompted a long-standing conflict between those who argue that the business of psychology, as of other natural sciences, is to *explain*, and those who maintain that it is to enable us to *understand*, human experience. In this context neither 'explain' nor 'understand' has ever been properly defined.

Apart from this contrast there is a legitimate sense in which psychology may be said to have a kinship with history and literature. The kinship with history is based on the fact that man has a history as well as a nature. The psychologist studies the life history of a particular person in a group, of his performance on any one occasion, of his total achievement or of his breakdown. Everything human not only has a personal, individual past; it also has a social past comprising all the influences that have impinged upon a person since his birth, apart from his genetic or ancestral history.

With respect to the kinship with literature it could be argued that a novelist or dramatist may and often does express thoughts about human character and motivation which are greatly revealing. Anyone who has read, say, Dostoevsky's *Crime and Punishment* or Samuel Butler's *The Way of all Flesh* must be deeply impressed by these writers' extraordinary insight into the human mind. It would be easy to list the names of a great many other authors equally gifted. Indeed, by comparison with the genius of Tolstoy, Stendhal, Flaubert, Proust or Thomas Mann, the ordinary textbook of psychology seems banal and commonplace. The intuition and imaginative powers of the man of letters undoubtedly give him an advantage over the experimental psychologist plodding away in the laboratory, or over the theorist meditating at his desk. He can probe profoundly into the human 'soul', depict situations and create characters in such a way as to enrich our minds and extend and expand the scope of our experience, understanding and sympathies. On the other hand, the psychologist, following the path of science, is privileged in a different way. He can present an intuition in a systematic and logical fashion, and he knows how to subject it to experiment and statistical test. He can bring to the problems of psychology the powerful tools of mathematics and logic, and knowledge gained in other sciences can be directly brought to bear on the issues that confront him.

In summing up, we can say that besides the tasks which it shares with other sciences, psychology carries an additional burden which it owes to the peculiar fact that its subject-matter has a double or twofold aspect: it is at once physical and mental. Hence explanations in psychology tend to be of two kinds, those that are expressed in terms of neurophysiology, and ultimately in the language of physics and chemistry, and those which are expressed in the natural language of everyday experience. These different languages are not, in principle, incompatible. They are supplementary. Psychology will remain incomplete until it can assimilate and integrate within a single system, what both, in their own ways, have to offer.*

Fig. 1 Place of psychology in the world of learning

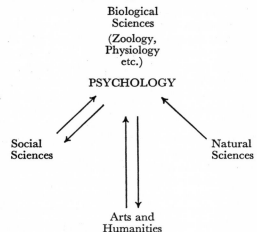

(Arrows indicate direction of flow of ideas and knowledge.)

Suggested Reading

COHEN, J., *A New Introduction to Psychology*, London: Allen & Unwin, 1966.

HEARNSHAW, L. S., *A Short History of British Psychology*, London: Methuen, 1964.

MILLER, G. A., *Psychology: The Science of Mental Life*, New York: Harper, 1962.

Mind of Man, London: The Grolier Society, 1968.

SUMMERFIELD, A. (ed.), *Experimental Psychology*, British Medical Bulletin, London: British Council, 1964.

ZANGWILL, O., *An Introduction to Modern Psychology*, London: Methuen, 1962.

* In the diagram which follows (Fig. 1), an attempt is made to indicate how psychology is related to the arts and sciences.

2

Physiological Psychology

Neville Moray

Introduction

One of the most rapidly progressing fields of psychology today is *physiological psychology*. This is the study of the relation between our experiences and behaviour, our feelings and desires on the one hand, and the physical structure of the body, especially the brain, on the other.

Many people still talk as if 'the body' and 'the mind' were two separate parts of a human being. But whether you choose to talk that way, or whether you believe that it is better to think of the two as different aspects of the single nature of man, there is no doubt that the mechanisms of the brain are crucially important for understanding the natural history which characterises a human being. Whatever you think about minds, souls and bodies, it is the mechanism of the brain through which we are able to have experiences and to do things. If you are hit on the head, the mechanical damage will put some parts of the brain temporarily out of action. If you receive a wound to the skull you may become paralysed or blind. If disease damages the cells which compose the brain, various sorts of malfunctioning may occur. These are all things which interfere with the normal functioning of the cells of which the brain consists, and by so doing interfere with the smooth functioning of its mechanism.

It is fashionable to compare the brain these days to a computer, and while there is frequently a lot of loose talk about this (for example, there are different kinds of computers with very different properties, and few people ever say to which sort they are comparing the brain), the analogy is fairly close for certain purposes. If you imagine the task of running to intercept a shot at tennis, when you see where the ball is going to be in a second or so, you must in fact calculate the path of the ball, and activate your muscles so as to move yourself and then the racket into the correct point in space. You do not, of course, work out an equation of motion consciously, but if you are to respond to an event which is about to take place and move in an appropriate way, then something in your brain, basing its response on past experience, must be making a calculation, for otherwise it would be hard to understand how you end up in the right place. We are beginning now to be able to make computers recognise patterns and learn to solve problems to which we do not know the answers, and as we deliberately build mechanisms to perform the behaviour which has always been associated with men, so we begin to get a feeling for the kind of problems faced by the mechanisms of the brain, and are able to begin to guess what the mechanisms may be.

To say that our experiences, feelings, desires and behaviour are performed by mechanism is not to belittle man. The brain may be a computer, but it is a unique one. It is a mechanism which in some way, of which we have no understanding, is able to be aware of what it is doing, to be self-conscious, to make decisions based on moral values as well as merely responding to stimulation. Our brain is a mechanism, but it is a human mechanism.

The physiological psychologist therefore studies the structure and function of the brain, trying to understand the relation between what he sees from the outside as it were, and what he experiences from the inside, as the 'owner' of a brain. We know that we recognise objects, we respond to stimuli, we avoid sources of pain and danger, and seek out things which we require, such as food or water. In short, we are organisms which are adaptive. We live in an environment which is fundamentally hostile to us. We are often too hot or too cold, too hungry or too thirsty, damaged by bumping into things, or tired by physical or mental labour. Yet we survive, since by making use of the information about the world which we acquire through learning, and the means of response at our disposal, we adapt. The brain is an adaptive, self-maintaining mechanism. It takes in information about the outside world, and constructs a model of that world inside itself. Our memories and the skills and responses that we have learnt constitute a record of the world, together with a record of the objects, sights, sounds, etc., which we have encountered in the past. Hence, when a particular stimulus arrives, we can compare its nature with the stored model of the world, and by recognising it and relating its nature to some past occurrence we can benefit from past experience and respond appropriately to it on this new occasion.

The task of the brain is thus to take information from the world in all the many ways in which it arrives, as light waves, sound waves, chemical stimuli and physical pressures, to translate this information into a form which is useful to the brain and which allows the sight, sound and feel of each thing to be recognised, and to organise appropriate responses on the basis of past experience. There are, to all intents and purposes, few if any instincts in human beings, few important inborn sets of responses to particular stimuli which may occur. In man, almost everything has to be learnt.

If we look at a brain superficially, there is not much to be seen. Its consistency is something like that of a caramel custard. It is covered with folds and bumps, and several nerves can be seen to run into it from the eyes, the ears and, by means of the spinal cord, from distant regions of the body. If we cut it open we can see, even with the naked eye, that it is not uniform in structure, and appropriate staining methods reveal that a large part of it seems to be made up of bundles of fibres which run from one region of the brain to another. The most obvious structures are the two 'hemispheres'. These are covered with a layer of cells, all richly connected to one another, the layer being only a few millimetres deep, but containing none the less many millions of cells. Each region of this layer (the cerebral cortex) is connected to other regions by the tracts of fibres, which in fact consist of the outgrowths of nerve cells, and along which pass information, as we shall see later on. But in addition to the cerebral cortex, we can see that there are other groups of cells buried deep in the brain, and these 'nuclei' as they are called, are connected with one another and also with the cells of the cortex. The general picture, then, is of regions where there are groups of cells connected with one another locally, and which therefore may be expected to have a function in common, together with pathways of nerve fibres which join the nuclei one to another, allowing the particular task which each performs to be integrated with the tasks performed by the others. The actual size of the individual cells is extremely small. The body of the cell is of the order of one-hundredth of a millimetre or less across, but the axon, the long fibre which carries the information from one part of the nervous system to another, may be many feet long, such as the nerve fibres which bring information about touch from the skin on the foot of, say, a giraffe to its spinal cord and hence to the brain.

We already know a great deal about the organisation of the brain. There are parts concerned with perception, with motivation, with sleep and wakefulness, with emotion and so on. In this chapter all we can do is to touch on a few of these functions and see how they are represented physically in the brain.

Motivation

We have said that the brain is an adaptive mechanism concerned with maintaining the person to whom it belongs in a healthy state. Obviously, the first requirement is to see that adequate amounts of food and drink are taken, for upon an adequate supply of energy and the correct concentration of the fluids of the body depends the healthy functioning of the whole organism. Most of the experiments which are performed directly on the brain are performed on animals, since although there is not nowadays much danger associated with operations on the brain, there is enough to make it unacceptable to interfere with a human brain except when it is absolutely necessary. But the structure of the brains of different species of animals are clearly related by the course which evolution has taken, so that we can find equivalent structures in the brains of different species.

There are several ways in which we may investigate the function of any part of the brain. We may remove the part in question, and see if the animal's behaviour is altered (the *ablation* or *lesion* technique). Frequently this provides very striking results. For example, if a region in the hypothalamus (one of the collections of cells deep in the middle of the brain) is damaged, the animal will cease to eat and will eventually starve to death, while removal of another region close to the former, results in over-eating until the animal becomes huge and obese. But the trouble with the ablation technique is that the results are always ambiguous. If you tear out almost any wire from the inside of a television set you will damage the quality of the picture, and may even lose it altogether, but this does not mean that the wire in question was causing the picture. It may have been controlling another part of the set which itself makes the picture, or just carrying electrical current from one part of the set to another to supply the power needed. Similarly, the result of a lesion shows that the part of the brain is involved in some way with the function in question, but not that it is the *centre* of that function.

A second method is to stimulate the cells. The nature of the messages which nerve cells pass from one to another is electrical, as we shall shortly see in more detail. Consequently, if we apply a very small electrical current to the part of the brain in which we are interested, we can make the cells unusually active. In the regions of the hypothalamus which we have mentioned, we find that stimulating that part the loss of which leads to starving makes the animal eat, and stimulating the part the loss of which leads to over-eating will make the animal stop eating, even if very hungry. In both instances the effect only lasts for the time that we are applying the electrical current to the part of the brain concerned.

Other ways of stimulating the brain may be used in

special circumstances. For example, it has been known to physiologists for a long time that one of the factors concerned with hunger is the concentration of sugar in the blood; and a number of chemical compounds are known to circulate in the blood which are closely related to sugar. Although human beings frequently eat for pleasure or for social reasons rather than because they are hungry, they also show the basic behaviour which is common to other animals as well, in that when they are hungry they will seek food, and eat until they are no longer hungry. The idea therefore comes to mind that perhaps the brain is able to measure the concentration of sugar or one of its related compounds in the blood, and 'turn on' food-seeking behaviour when it becomes necessary. Experiments have been performed in which very tiny amounts of sugar solutions, or of compounds which alter the sugar concentration of the body fluids have been injected directly into the part of the hypothalamus which the other experiments have made us think is concerned with hunger; and although the exact compound concerned has not yet been identified, it does seem that when the blood-sugar level falls too low, then food-seeking behaviour begins. The nerve cells in the feeding centres of the hypothalamus send impulses to other regions of the brain, and the animal begins to move about the environment looking for food. Those parts of the brain where memories of past experience are stored will add their information to the organisation of the behaviour so that the hungry animal will visit places where in the past food has been found, and food when found will be eaten.

The control of even such simple behaviour as this, however, is very complicated. For example, while the fall in blood-sugar seems to start feeding, feeding stops long before the level is back to normal. Since it takes some time for food which is eaten to be digested and for the substances to be absorbed from the digestive system and to reach the blood, the animal must stop eating when enough food has been consumed to raise the blood-sugar level to its proper value sometime later when it has all been digested. So the brain is sensitive to several other factors: the flavour of the food (information reaches it from the tongue), the amount of bulk in the stomach (nerves carry messages from the stomach wall to the brain) and so on; and on the basis of this information feeding behaviour is turned off when the brain calculates that enough food has been consumed.

There is thus a delicate balance between the *motivation centres* (those parts of the hypothalamus which initiate and stop feeding), the *cortex* (to which the information from the sensory nerves of the tongue, eyes, etc., is taken) and the chemistry of the body; and all interact in such a way that the appropriate adaptive behaviour is shown by the animal as a whole. A pictorial model of this system is shown in Fig. 1.

Other motivation mechanisms are also known to have control centres in this part of the brain. These centres can be shown to be involved in the same kind of interaction between the internal and external world as those which characterise the hunger centres. In one experiment, the hypothalamus of a goat was stimulated electrically, and drinking continued until the animal had drunk nearly three gallons of water. The usual stimulus in this instance seems to be the concentration of inorganic salts such as sodium chloride in the blood. The body fluids in which all cells are bathed, and of which all cells are composed, need to be kept at the correct concentration for the body to function. If a lot of water is lost, perhaps through sweating on a hot day or during exercise, the concentration of these salts and other substances rises, and in order to restore the correct amount of fluid the animal will drink. If small amounts of salt solution are injected into the hypothalamus, drinking ensues, just as injections of appropriate substances cause feeding behaviour. Dryness in the mouth is alleviated by water passing through the mouth and down the throat, and messages are sent from cells in the tongue to the brain to estimate how much, and what kind of fluid has been drunk. In some species there are special cells which detect the presence of salt or of pure water, and just as the intake of food is cut off before the actual tissues are restored, so drinking is turned off by these messages about what is being drunk. The mechanisms can, in fact, be 'tricked', since if an operation is performed so that the water never reaches the stomach of the animal, but is allowed to re-emerge from a tube in the throat, it will stop drinking after an appropriate amount of water has passed through the mouth. It will, however, begin drinking again sooner than a normal animal.

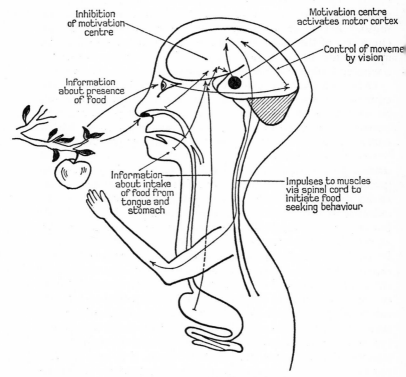

Fig. 1 Control of feeding behaviour

Perception

In the above description of how the brain initiates behaviour which is suited to achieve the biological needs of the organism we have glossed over several points. We said, for example, that the hungry animal would seek out places where it had found food before, and would recognise food objects associated with it. But how does it do this? Let us now look at the mechanisms by which perception is mediated in the nervous system.

Every organism is 'bathed' in information. Patterns of light, of sound, bumps, touches, smells and tastes constantly arrive at the surface of the body. And these patterns carry information about the kinds of objects which are in the vicinity of an organism at any moment. The actual physical nature of the information is very different for the different senses. Light energy and sound energy have very different properties, and smell and taste may be due to the chemical nature of the objects rather than the physical nature of the energy. But all alike convey, or can convey, to the animal information about the world.

This information can be thought of as reaching the organism in different languages. Light speaks of the colour, shape and brightness of an object. Sound speaks of its loudness, whether it is speech or just noise. But it is clear that to the human or other organism these languages are often the same in effect. If you have taught someone to respond to the word CAT in an experiment, a similar response will be given (although probably less strongly) to the sight of a cat or to the touch of a cat.

The brain appears to translate this information in the languages of the different sense modalities into the one common language of the nervous system, the language of the nerve cell. And once this translation has been made the comparison and integration of the messages arriving through the different senses can occur.

There are many more than the five traditional senses. We should at least add the sense of balance, of muscle tension and limb position to the list, and probably others as well. All have certain features in common. To begin with, each sense has a group of specialised cells called *receptors*, which use the physical energy arriving from the outside world to initiate nerve impulses. They are nerve cells, but special nerve cells. Thus in the eye the rod and cone cells of the retina contain pigment, so that when light strikes the eye it is absorbed by the pigment which thus gains the energy of the light waves. This changes the chemical properties of the cell so that it sends an impulse to the other cells with which it is connected, and hence the message about the presence of light is sent on its way to the brain. In the ear, by contrast, sound waves which arrive are made to send a wave of pressure through the fluid which fills the inner ear, and this affects special cells which are sensitive to mechanical deformation. They therefore fire, and send the messages on their way to the part of the brain concerned with hearing.

Rather than take a brief look at each sense in turn, we shall consider the sense of hearing and look closely at what is known about its organisation in the brain. In this way we will be able to get a feeling of the kind of research which is at present going on to understand the physical basis of mental events. We must begin by discussing in more detail than we have yet done the precise nature of the 'nerves' and 'nerve cells' (or *neurons* as they are often called).

Figure 2 shows a typical nerve cell. Nerve cells are found in a great variety of shapes and sizes, but most of them exhibit the same parts as are shown in the figure. The *cell body* contains the nucleus of the cell and, together with the short branches called *dendrites*, is the region where the end feet of other nerve cells finish. The *axon*, which may have many branches, connects the cell body with other nerve cells, which may be near by (as happens with cells within a single nucleus of the brain), or they may be a long distance away (as in the nerves which run to and from the spinal cord and the skin and muscles). The function of a nerve cell is to pass information from one part of the brain to another and it is the arrival of this information and its impact on what is going on in the brain at the time which goes to make our experiences and to bring about the organisation of our behaviour. The nature of the message is very simple. When a stimulus of sufficient strength arrives at the body or dendrites of the cell, a small pulse of electricity travels down the axon to the endfeet of the cell where, if conditions are right, it will cause the next nerve cell to fire in its turn, or if it is connected to a muscle, will cause the muscle to contract thus tending to produce bodily movement.

This transmission of small pulses of electricity along the length of the cell is the only thing which most nerve

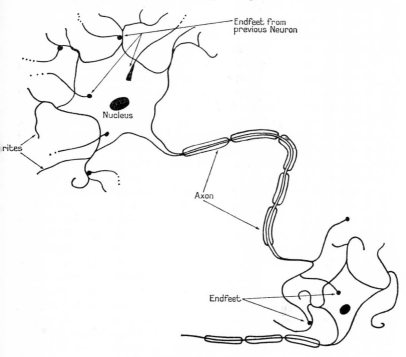

Fig. 2 The Nerve Cell

cells can do. This is the basic word in the language of the nervous system, a message which tells the next cell 'I have been stimulated'. There is no difference, so far as we know, between the pulses which a neuron in the visual system transmits and those which a cell in the auditory system transmits. The only difference is their origin and the pathways over which they run. Thus if a cell in the visual system fires, it implies that earlier on a receptor cell in the eye was stimulated by light. If a cell in the auditory pathway fires it implies that earlier on one of the sound receptor cells fired and passed the message on, and that therefore there was probably a noise in the vicinity of the listener. But if we simply looked at a nerve cell by itself, without knowing whether it was one in the chain of cells from the eye or from the ear, we could not tell what sort of information was being carried.

Once the receptors have done their job of transforming the physical energy into the nerve impulse, it is in a form which is common throughout the brain, and it becomes fairly easy to understand how a pattern of impulses which represents the mewing of a cat, say, can come to be connected with the pattern representing the sight of a cat. Neither pattern is very similar to the stimulus which caused it, but they are in comparable codes and so can be related by the brain.

Another example of the common language of the nervous system is the way in which the strength of a stimulus is measured. If we stimulate a single nerve cell with an electrical current of gradually increasing strength, we find that as we increase the strength of the stimulus nothing seems to happen at first. Then suddenly the pulse of electricity appears, the cell 'fires', and the pulse, lasting about 1/1000 second, travels down the nerve fibre at a speed of some hundred feet a second. If we go on increasing the strength of the stimulus, we find that it makes no difference to the size of the nervous impulse. It does not get bigger. This, the 'all-or-none law', is sometimes compared to the firing of a gun. If you squeeze the trigger very gently, nothing happens. If you squeeze it hard enough it will fire the gun, but even if you squeeze it very much harder, it will not make the bullet go any faster. Similarly, once the threshold of the nerve cell is reached, the strength of the stimulus makes no difference to the size of the impulse.

Hence there must be some other way in which the intensity of a stimulus is represented. We can certainly experience differences in intensity. One light looks brighter than another; one fire feels warmer than another; so that some-how the translation of intensity into neural impulses must be done.

In fact, use is made of a *frequency code*. Regardless of whether we are dealing with light, sound, pressure or tem-perature, the stronger the stimulus the more frequently the pulses follow one another down the nerve fibre. The strength of a stimulus is translated by the nerve cells into the fre-quency with which they fire. Hence once the receptors have performed the initial translation, there is a great deal in common between the equivalent aspects of the different physical stimuli as received by the brain.

The number of nerve cells is enormously large. It is usually said that there are about 10,000,000,000 nerve cells in the mature brain. And any single 'nerve', as the word is popularly used (to mean, for example, the nerve which runs from the eye to the brain), contains many hundreds of thousands of nerve fibres. The great tracts of fibres which we see when we cut into the brain are, in fact, bundles of the axons of cells, the bodies of which are in the cortex or in the nuclei, and if we trace their paths from the receptors in the sense organs to the brain we find that we can map the brain into different regions which seem to be concerned with different functions.

Since the nature of the messages is electrical, we can record the small currents which occur when nerve cells fire, and thus it is possible to discover which regions of the brain are active when the different kinds of sensory stimuli occur. The main distinctions between regions of the cortex are shown in Fig. 3. We shall now consider in more detail the region concerned with hearing.

Sound enters the external ear and is conducted by the chain of bones attached to the inner surface of the eardrum to the receptor cells in the inner ear. Here the energy of the sound wave makes a pressure wave travel through the fluid with which the inner ear is filled. The receptor organ is called the *cochlea* (from the Latin word for a shell, because of its shape), and contains a membrane made of elastic tissue, which bulges under the pressure wave which the sound causes. The bulge caused by the pressure grows bigger and then smaller as it travels along the membrane, and the place where it is at its biggest varies for notes of different frequen-

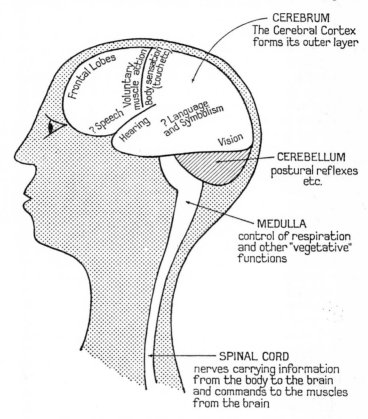

Fig. 3 The Organisation of the Nervous System

cies, so that the cochlea acts as a device for measuring the pitch of the incoming sound. It probably acts by breaking up complex sound waves into their components to some extent; and then, since the receptor cells are arranged along the length of the cochlea, the message sent to the brain

34

represents sounds of different pitch according to which groups of cells fired, cells farthest into the cochlea firing to low-pitched notes and those nearer the beginning signalling the occurrence of high notes.

From the cochlea messages are sent along the *auditory nerve* to the brain itself. This nerve ends in the *cochlear nucleus*, the first of a series of relay stations which form a chain of cells all the way from the ear to the *auditory cortex*. Since we know that nerve cells can be much longer than this, why are there these relays instead of just one nerve fibre running straight to the brain? The answer is that various things are done to the messages on the way to the brain. The synapse, the place where one nerve cell ends and the next begins, is the only place where messages can interact. Hence these relay points represent places at which some change occurs in the message. For example, at the cochlear nucleus certain features of the message are made more distinct. Although the frequency of the incoming sound is represented by the region of the cochlea which is most strongly stimulated, there is tremendous overlap. A loud low-pitched sound, for example, will throw most of the cochlea into activity, so that on the basis of the analysis by the cochlear alone we would not be able to distinguish many different sounds. At the cochlear nucleus, the messages interact to sharpen the boundaries between them. A similar effect occurs in vision, where at a light/dark boundary the dark side seems darker and the bright side brighter immediately on either side of the boundary.

Furthermore, there is the very important problem of how we tell from what direction sounds are coming. Quite apart from the problem of identifying the source of a sound, and thus, for example, being warned about the presence of a car which we cannot see about to come around a corner, we make a great deal of use of the direction of sounds when listening to people talk. In a crowd at a party where many people are talking at once, it is our ability to block messages arriving from directions other than from the person to whom we are listening that allows us selectively to pay attention to only one person. Since sound travels at about 1 foot every thousandth of a second, there will be a slight difference in the time of arrival of a sound at the two ears if the sound source is out to one side; and there will also be slight differences in loudness between the messages received by the two ears because of the 'shadow' caused by the head. These very small differences—of the order of fractions of a thousandth of a second—are used by the brain to measure the direction from which sound comes and so we find pathways by which this comparison is carried out, joining the nerves from the two sides of the brain. Furthermore, if we record the electrical activity from the two sides of the brain at each level at which there is a synapse, we find that if two sounds arrive one at each ear with a slight delay between them, the earlier sound actually suppresses the response of the nervous system to the later one, suggesting that here again there is a sharpening of the differences between stimuli.

In this way, by recording with extremely fine electrodes all the way up the auditory pathway, we can attempt to map the function which each level of the nervous system performs on the messages as they sweep inwards and upwards from the ear to the auditory cortex. We also find that there are pathways running in the opposite directions, which are probably responsible for sending messages downwards from the cortex to control the flow of messages coming in, and which therefore may be part of the mechanism by which we pay attention to one message and ignore another.

Although there is still a great deal to be learnt before the whole mechanism is understood, we are beginning to get a picture of how the auditory system is organised. Two maps of it are shown in Figs. 4 and 5. In one is shown the anatomy of the brain, with the pathways running up and down between the cortex and the peripheral sense organs in the ear. In the other is shown something of what we know about the functions performed by the different nuclei. The incoming pathway ends at the cortex, which is the part of the brain which is more and more highly developed the higher up the evolutionary scale we come, so that it is fair to expect it to be concerned with the most complex performances of the organism. In fact, it seems that without the cortex the dis-

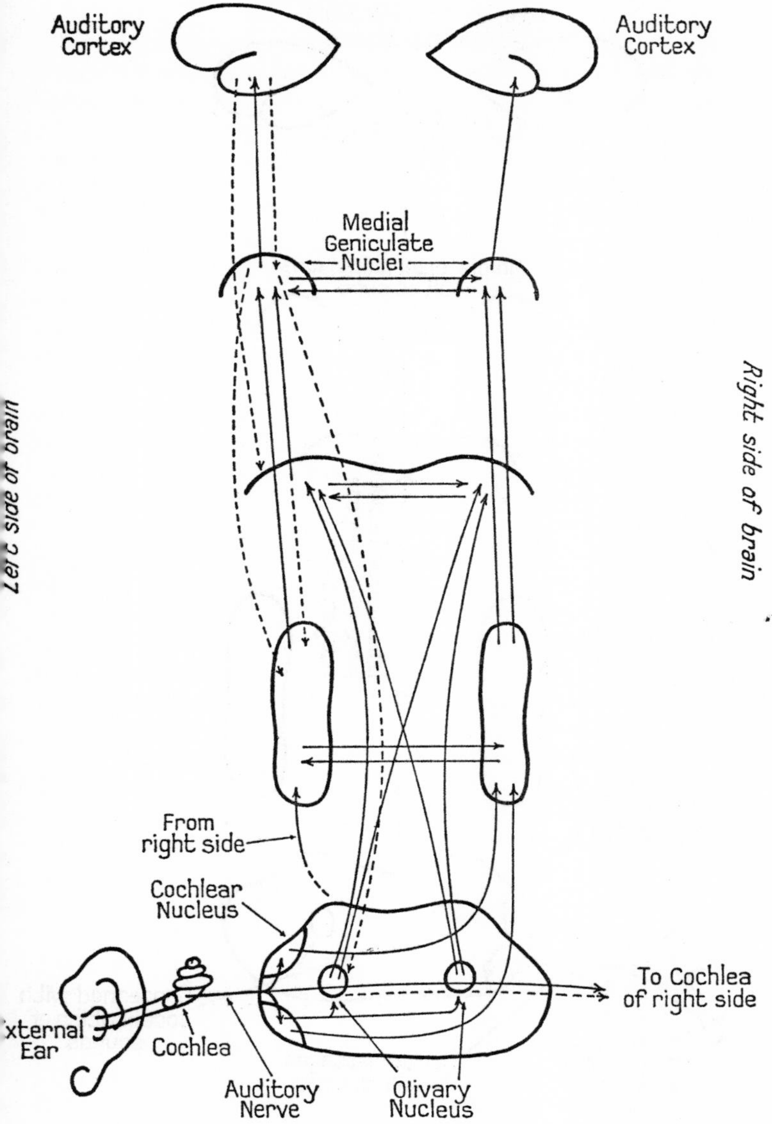
Auditory Cortex
Auditory Cortex
Medial Geniculate Nuclei
side of brain
Right side of brain
From right side
Cochlear Nucleus
To Cochlea of right side
xternal
Ear
Cochlea
Auditory Nerve
Olivary Nucleus

Fig. 4 The Brain: structure

D

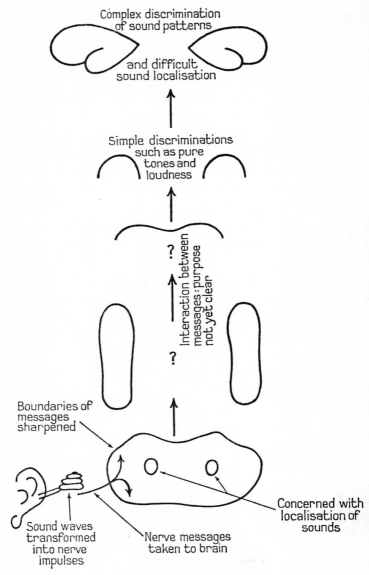

Complex discrimination
of sound patterns

and difficult
sound localisation

Simple discriminations
such as pure
tones and
loudness

Interaction between
messages: purpose
not yet clear

?

?

Boundaries of
messages
sharpened

Concerned with
localisation of
sounds

Sound waves
transformed
into nerve
impulses

Nerve messages
taken to brain

Fig. 5 The Brain: organisation

crimination of complex patterns of sound is impossible. In one experiment, after the removal of the auditory cortex (that part of the cortex to which the information about sound finally comes) a cat was found to be unable to distinguish patterns of high and low notes. It could not differentiate between a sequence of notes which went high–low–high from one which went low–high–low, although it was still almost as sensitive as a normal animal to the task of distinguishing the occurrence of a single tone from silence. In other words, the cat was not deaf, but it could not distinguish patterns. Similarly in vision, an animal which has lost the part of the cortex which is concerned with vision cannot distinguish one shape from another, but can detect the presence or absence of light.

One of the most exciting recent developments has deepened our understanding of the role of the cortex in interpreting patterns. Both in vision and in hearing there have been found groups of cells which respond to particular aspects of the stimulus. Thus in the auditory cortex some cells only fire in response to a note of rising pitch, others to one of falling pitch. In vision some only fire to a horizontal line in the visual field, others only to a vertical line; some to a light shone in both eyes, but not to one shone in only one eye. And these details can be related to the behaviour of the animals. For example, some species can tell the following two patterns apart:

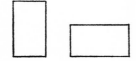

but not these:

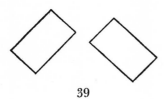

Other species can perform both discriminations, and it seems that the latter have groups of cells which fire to slanting patterns, while the former do not. The next ten or twenty years will probably enable us to understand almost completely how our perception of patterns and objects in the world is achieved by the brain.

Emotion

Our perception of the world and the objects which it contains is usually remarkably accurate, and through such methods as the *constancies* mechanisms of the brain tend to make perception not merely accurate but also adaptive. That is, we see things in a way which can be used most efficiently in organising our responses to them. It would be awkward if we saw people who were approaching us at first as very small, and then becoming bigger and bigger. In fact, our brains make allowance for their distance from us, so that normally we see a person we know as being that person, and not just someone who looks like him but is much smaller.

In a similar way, we keep a record of the emotional colouring of our past experiences, so that in perception objects and people are not merely identified as to who and what they are, but also in terms of the emotional response which they cause in us. This has obvious advantages. There are a number of things which are dangerous, and which it is important for us to respond to even if we are initially paying attention to something else. In man's primitive state there were many more, such as the animals which hunted him. And reflecting on the primitive origins of emotion, we can see that many if not all the situations which arouse fear or anger in a person or an animal are also ones in which some more or less violent response is called for. In fearful situations primitive man would have to be ready to run for his life, or to fight for it. And this would require the appropriate bodily changes. More oxygen would have to be sent to the muscles, more waste products carried away, breathing would have to be modified, and all the extensive alterations in the chemistry and functioning of the body would have to be initiated in response not to every object perceived, but to a certain class of what we may call 'emotionally important' perceptions.

Perception, then, can lead to alteration in the state of the body, and we might surmise that these changes are in some way linked to the actual feelings, such as anger, which we experience when we perceive certain objects. But, likewise, our emotions can alter the way in which we respond to the information which reaches our sense organs.

When Freud developed his theory of personality, he included the provision for what we now call 'perceptual defence', whereby we unconsciously detect the presence of forbidden or unpleasant stimuli; this makes it impossible or at least much more difficult to perceive such stimuli. Whether there is such a mechanism, and whether it works in the way which psychoanalysts suggest, is extremely doubtful. But we are able in certain situations to show the importance of emotionally toned stimuli. For example, it is commonly thought that we are more sensitive to our own name than to anyone else's. To test this we can perform the following experiment. We ask a subject to wear a pair of headphones, and then play two speech messages to him, one through his left ear and one through his right ear. His task is to repeat the message which he receives through his right ear while he hears it and to ignore the message in his left ear. Included in the middle of the rejected message is the phrase: 'All right, you may stop now.' He will not hear the message, and will not stop. But if we change that part of the rejected message to include his own name, 'John Smith, you may stop now,' he will very frequently hear it. Another experiment is more spectacular. A person goes to sleep with recording electrodes placed on his head, so that we can record the electrical rhythms of his brain through the skull while he sleeps. If we now play tape-recordings of names to him, he is more likely to wake to his own name than to other names. But also, we can see changes in the brain rhythms, corresponding to the beginning of arousal, more frequently to his own name than to other names even when he does not wake up and when he is not aware of having heard any names at all. That is, our brains respond to emotionally important stimuli more strongly than to others, even when we are not aware of what is going on.

In this second experiment we are picking up direct evidence of the activity of physical mechanisms connected with emotion. In fact, there are certain nervous mechanisms which are closely linked to the emotional response. Thus we can record electrical changes in the skin. When a person gets a sudden shock, is startled, or is emotionally upset, the electrical resistance of his skin alters, as a result of activity in the sweat glands of the skin. The resistance falls, and this change can be measured by suitable recording instruments. The change is not due to water being released in the form of sweat but to electrical changes in the glands themselves which make the sweat. In the second experiment to which I have just referred and in which the subjects were asleep, one student persistently gave enormous galvanic skin responses (or G.S.R. as these changes are called) to the name 'Penelope', showing that the name caused an emotional arousal in him even when he was fast asleep; and when he awoke at the end of the experiment, it turned out that the subject (who was actually the writer of this chapter, at the time a medical student) had taken a new girl-friend of that name to a dance for the first time on the previous evening.

The galvanic skin response is used in certain practical applications, such as the so-called 'lie detector'. The suspect is asked a series of questions while his G.S.R. is recorded, and the theory is that when he is asked a question to do with the crime he is suspected of having committed he will lie, and the emotional stress of lying will cause a change in the G.S.R. The objection to the method is obvious—the changes are a measure of any emotional arousal, not just of lying. But it is possibly a helpful device for narrowing down the range of suspects, and is used extensively in certain countries by the police, although not in Britain.

The nervous mechanisms which are involved in the

activity of the sweat glands are part of a whole section of the nervous system which we have not so far mentioned, and which is called the *autonomic nervous system*. The autonomic nervous system is concerned with the control and response of the internal environment of the body rather than with the processing of information about the external environment which surrounds the organism. Thus under autonomic control are such things as the secretion of digestive juices, the contraction and expansion of blood vessels. For example, during exercise blood vessels in the muscles open up and those to the gut shut down, thus making more blood available for carrying oxygen to the muscles; sweating takes place so as to alter the rate at which heat produced by muscle action is lost; and the heart rate is increased. In brief, the autonomic system regulates the 'vegetative' functions of the body, ensuring that the maintenance of the biological machinery is suitable. It is this system which is very closely connected with the response to emotional stimulation. In response to fear or excitement not only does the G.S.R. occur, which, as we have seen, is connected with sweating, but in addition the heart rate alters, the blood pressure changes, and other physiological and chemical changes occur throughout the body. The nervous system normally causes its effects directly by transmitting impulses from one nerve cell to another, or by making a muscle contract. But there is a third way in which the nervous system can cause a response in some distant part of the body, and that is by means of *hormones*. Certain glands in the body produce chemicals which exert a powerful action on other bodily tissues. Thus the *adrenal gland*, a small organ located close to the kidney, liberates a substance called *adrenalin* when signals from the autonomic nervous system reach it. Adrenalin is very closely involved in the so-called 'fight or flight reflex', which prepares the body for violent action in response to emotional arousal. It stimulates the heart and alters the degree of dilation of the blood vessels, and it is such chemical responses to autonomic stimulation which give rise to many of the sensations which go with violent emotion. 'Butterflies in the stomach' are partly

43

caused by contractions of the gut, and the heart may pound in response to adrenalin. And since the secretion of the powerful digestive juices is also under autonomic control, the connexion between mental worry and physical illness such as an ulcerated stomach becomes intelligible. A constant state of worry and excitement will activate the autonomic nervous system, and the digestive juices will be liberated at times when there is no food to be digested, with the result that there may be damage to the lining of the stomach. In addition, the blood flow to the organs of the body may be altered in a maladaptive way by adrenalin output. The functioning of the nervous system is very closely interlinked with that of the other chemical systems of the body.

This being so, we should expect to be able to interfere with the mechanisms of emotion either by intervening with nervous function or more directly with the chemical functions themselves. We have recently discovered that there are parts of the brain which if removed make an animal prone to violent attacks of 'sham rage'. Even very slight stimuli which in a normal animal would only lead to a trivial response such as scratching or withdrawal induce violent attacks, the hair stands on end, and every sign of extreme rage occurs, although it is important to notice that it is emotional *behaviour*, not necessarily emotional *experience*, which we are causing. We are beginning to understand that there is a delicate balance between two systems in the brain, one of which produces intense emotional excitement and the other which inhibits the response, so that it is possible both to make an animal unusually violent or unusually placid by appropriate brain surgery. One particularly interesting change following an operation on the brain, and one that is very difficult to understand, sometimes follows an operation on the frontal lobes of the brain (Fig. 3). In the early days of operations on this region, very extensive changes in the personality of the patients often used to be seen. But with the more refined techniques now used, such adverse effects are comparatively rare. The operation is sometimes performed to relieve pain when it is very severe and when other operations have failed or are impossible. And in such instances, the patients, when asked how they feel, sometimes say, 'Oh, the pain is just as bad as it was, but I don't mind it any more.' It is very puzzling to know what to make of this, but since there are pathways from the frontal lobes to the parts of the brain concerned with elaborating the emotional responses to stimuli, it may be that in some way the emotional value of the pain, 'what pain is worth', or 'what it means' to the patient, has been altered.

It is presumably by interfering with the arousal system and the emotional system of the brain that drugs such as tranquillisers and stimulants produce their effects. Although we said earlier that there is not very much difference between the different kinds of nerve cells, there are certain differences which, while not visible in their structure directly, must none the less be present at the microscopic level. For example, some parts of the brain take up certain stains more readily than others, some cells have thicker walls on their axons, and more than one kind of chemical are liberated at the end feet. Hence it is reasonable to suppose that when a person takes a drug some parts of the brain may be affected by it more than others. There is much research at present into the way in which drugs affect only one part of the brain and not others. A good example is the way in which travel sickness pills all affect the parts of the brain concerned with vomiting and the response to the messages from the receptors serving the sense of balance, but some, in addition, make people feel very sleepy, presumably by acting on the arousal system.

Chemistry and Behaviour

The relation between drugs and behaviour, and the possibility of manipulating behaviour and experience by means of chemicals brings us in a sense back to the problem with which we began this chapter, the control of motivational and appetitive behaviour. There, it will be recalled, we saw that it is the concentration of certain substances in the blood which initiate feeding and drinking behaviour. And this important link between chemical and neural control of behaviour is shown by the whole *endocrine system*. Several glands in the body produce hormones, chemicals which affect the functioning of other bodily organs and also, in some instances behaviour. Among these are the thyroid gland and also the glands of the reproductive system in addition to the adrenal gland already mentioned. In all these glands there is a very elegant system whereby the concentration of the hormones is kept at the level which promotes the most efficient functioning of the body.

The thyroid gland surrounds the larynx in the neck and releases into the blood a hormone which controls the general level of metabolism in the body. If the concentration of this hormone rises excessively, the person becomes overactive, may be unable to sleep and may have hallucinations. If it falls too low, the efficiency of the body will be impaired in another way, for the rate at which the cells operate will become too slow. Eventually the brain will become inefficient, and the person will appear dull and be unable to think properly. At the base of the brain is a gland which produces a hormone which stimulates the thyroid gland to produce thyroid hormone, and when the concentration of thyroid hormone falls too low, this gland produces more thyroid stimulating hormone. The rising concentration of thyroid hormone causes the output of this other gland to fall, and so the system keeps itself in balance. An unforgettable if slightly fanciful account of the effect of thyroid deficiency on behaviour can be found in Dorothy L. Sayers' novel *Hangman's Holiday*, in a story called 'The Incredible Elopement of Lord Peter Wimsey', which also includes an account of how normal function can be restored by suitably treating the patient with supplies of hormone provided artificially in the diet.

Similarly, the reproductive cycle is very closely controlled by a combination of hormonal and neural factors. In female animals the time of the onset of heat and the readiness to mate are controlled by a series of hormones. When the hormone cycle reaches a particular phase, the female is willing to mate, and only then becomes sensitive to the mating behaviour patterns of the male: and in a similar way the female becomes more stimulating to the male when she is at the appropriate part of the cycle. Mating behaviour can be brought on at other times by injecting small quantities of hormones into certain brain centres which control the mating behaviour. But where the sex hormones are concerned there is a particularly subtle relation between the neural and hormonal control mechanisms. Mating on the part of an animal involves a series of responses to stimuli which are outside it. The mating partner must be recognised, and approached. The correct behaviour patterns must be initiated, the correct responses must be made, and the final mating involves complex behaviour on the part of both creatures. Although the time of mating in lower animals is under close control of the hormone level, and although the behaviour patterns involved are instinctive and hardly varied, nonetheless there is always some improvement in the efficiency of mating behaviour with practice, showing that there is at least a small part of the behaviour which is learnt, and therefore determined by neural, not hormonal, influences. As we ascend the evolutionary series we find that the neural element becomes increasingly important, the hormonal level less so. Among monkeys and apes we find that sexual behaviour occurs even when the female is not on heat, and, provided that they have had sexual experience beforehand, male animals still show most of the patterns of sexual behaviour after castration, which causes the production of male sex hormone to cease. Finally, in man there is virtually complete emancipation from hormonal control. Behaviour is no longer inborn but has to be learnt in the light of social convention, and by far the most important elements in the control of sexual behaviour are the neural mechanisms of learning and decisions. Samuel Butler once said that a hen is just one egg's way of making another egg. But in man the change from instinctive and hormonal control means that there is not the compulsion to reproductive behaviour such as we observe in other species. Man can use his sexual behaviour to express his love, rather than being used by it—the triumph of the neural mechanisms of learning over the more primitive chemical mechanisms and instinct.

Learning and Memory

Having raised the problem of learning, we must now look at the physical mechanisms which underlie it. Man is, above all, the animal who learns. Of instincts, the complex patterns of behaviour, inborn and released by specific stimuli, producing specific responses, there is not much more than a trace. Instead of relying on instinct, man takes the more perilous but more promising pathway of adaptation by learning.

At birth the behavioural repertory of a human baby is extremely limited. As the years go by, a staggering richness of response to the world around becomes evident. Languages are learnt, a range of physical skills acquired, behaviour patterns fitted to the particular social milieu of the child absorbed and then altered as the child passes through school, leaves home and moves into new social surroundings. Objects which were originally meaningless come to have value, new ideas and actions are discovered and incorporated into the behavioural and experiential world of the individual. All these events must be accompanied by, be carried by, physical changes in the organisation of the nerve cells in the brain—the physical basis of memory and learning.

Despite the enormous importance of learning and memory, their mechanism remains largely a mystery. The brain is immensely complex, and the changes which occur when we learn and remember something seem to be peculiarly elusive. The last few years have seen notable advances in many areas of physiological psychology, but comparatively little has been achieved in the growth of our understanding of memory. Again and again experiments are reported by scientists which seem to be opening up new avenues of research, but all of them have so far remained unsuccessful, and the physical basis of memory seems likely to be the

hardest of all the problems to solve in our efforts to understand the organisation of our brains.

Some things do, however, seem clear. There is some
difference between the way in which memories are stored
just after we have had an experience and storage after some
delay. For example, people who have suffered concussion,
perhaps as a result of a motor-cycle accident in which the
head receives a violent blow, generally have a large gap in
their memory for the events preceding the crash. This gap
may initially extend over several days, but the earlier
memories, those which refer to events many hours before
the accident gradually return, until some time later only
the record of events for the last few minutes or seconds
before the crash is missing. And of these there is a short
period just before the blow on the head which is never
remembered. Similarly, if electric shock is given to the
brain, as may be done in the treatment of some kinds of
mental illness, the events just before the moment of the
shock are not recalled. And in experiments on animals, if
they receive shocks to the brain just after they have been
rewarded for performing a task, they will not learn, whereas
a delay of several minutes between reward and shock allows
them to learn.

It seems, then, that the physical changes take some time
to occur if a stable memory is to be laid down. We find
in other instances of brain damage, due to disease, or sometimes to accidents, or physical deterioration due to damage
such as may be incurred over the years in boxing, that
sometimes people can remember things for a few minutes,
providing they are not distracted, but seem unable to transfer them to the long-lasting, stable kind of memory—the
connexion between short- and long-term memory is lost.
Similar effects may occur as a result of ageing.

On the other hand, memories once laid down seem extra
ordinarily resistant to damage. Shock or concussion very
rarely permanently removes memories which have existed
for some time. And despite the fact that brain cells are lost
throughout life at the rate of some 100,000 a day, the
memories of old people for events which happened early in

their youth can be extraordinarily rich and accurate. The effects of damage on long-term memory seem rather slight. And there do not seem to be particular areas of the brain where damage causes specific loss of memory. One gets the impression that, unlikely though it may appear, memories are not located in any particular part of the brain, unlike the motivation centres and other faculties which we have looked at. There is one area of the brain where stimulation can sometimes make people appear to re-live experiences, so that they hear tunes, and see people and events. But even in this instance there is not enough evidence for us to say that this is *the* place where memories are stored.

Since to learn to produce a new piece of behaviour to an old stimulus, or to link a new stimulus to some previously learnt pattern of behaviour involves changing the way in which the nerve cells act upon one another, we must try to find properties of the cells which might be related to these changes. Again, one or two are known, but not enough to give a clear picture. It seems that the more often one cell stimulates another the more easy it is for it to continue to do so, and intuitively this would seem to provide the kind of mechanism which could be the basis of practice improving performance. Again, there is a part of the brain which causes very rapid learning when it is stimulated. If an experiment is arranged so that whenever an animal presses a bar it stimulates that particular part of its brain, then it rapidly learns to press the bar, and will do so at an extremely high rate for hours at a time. Indeed, with this technique we can 'train' individual nerve cells or groups of nerve cells. We record the electrical activity of a single cell of the brain, and wait until it fires spontaneously. Immediately, we stimulate the 'reinforcement centre' just referred to. We repeat this each time the cell fires, and gradually it begins to fire more and more frequently. So here is a mechanism which seems in some way very closely connected with changing the properties of nerve cells in the living brain.

Very recent experiments have drawn our attention to the possible importance of chemical factors in memory. It has been found that the amount of RNA (a chemical which is closely related to DNA which stores the genetic information in genes) alters when cells are very active. And since a change in the way a cell interacts with its neighbours must be related to its chemistry, this observation and that on other changes in cell chemistry are very interesting. But these experiments are very difficult to conduct, and some of them have proved impossible to repeat by other scientists, and hence for the time being we cannot assess their true value.

This work on the physical basis of memory is an example of the way in which physiological psychology must now progress. The time when an individual worker, whether psychologist or physiologist, could single-handed hope to unravel these great problems is for the most part over. The future will see teams composed of physiologists, psychologists, chemists, and perhaps even engineers working together to ask different kinds of questions about the same phenomena. The psychologist will test the conscious person and animals to see what tasks they are capable of performing. The physiologist, neurologist and chemist will measure the properties of the microscopic mechanisms of the brain. And the newest recruit, the engineer, will perhaps work on modelling the brain and indeed the whole organism. For we have come to realise that the brain is a huge and complex network through which information, in the form of electrical impulses, flows. The engineers of today are beginning to understand the properties of such complex systems as they build computers and machines which adapt themselves to different conditions without the intervention of human beings and which show a sort of artificial intelligence, and they can make suggestions as to what kinds of systems might be embodied in the brain.

All in all, the next century looks like being the golden age of discovery into the physical basis of human personality in all its extraordinary richness, an age in which the only machine which is conscious of its own working, and which loves and hates, works and plays, thinks and dreams begins to understand how it is able to be—Man.

Suggested Reading

MUELLER, C. J., *Sensory Psychology*, New York: Prentice-Hall, 1965.
DETHIER, V. G., and STELLAR, E., *Animal Behaviour*, New York: Prentice-Hall, 1964.
WOOLDRIDGE, D. E., *The Machinery of the Brain*, New York: McGraw-Hill, 1963.
MORAY, N., *Cybernetics, Machines with Intelligence*, London: Burns Oates, 1963.
MORGAN, C. L., *Physiological Psychology*, New York: McGraw-Hill, 1965.
COOPERSMITH, F. (ed.), *Frontiers of Psychological Research*, London: W. H. Freeman, 1966.
MORAY, N., *Introduction to Psychology*, London: Blackies, 1967.

3
Experimental Psychology

Andrew H. Gregory

Introduction

The term 'experimental psychology' covers most of the areas
of psychology in which it is relatively easy to perform carefully controlled experiments. This includes topics such as
the study of perception, remembering, learning, problem-
solving, and the effects of emotion and motivation. In the
early days of psychology these studies were usually made in
the laboratory, but more recently the practical applications
of the subject have been developed, and the experimental
psychologist is now just as likely to be found studying aircraft pilots, car drivers or operators of industrial machinery.
He may be interested in studying the learning or practised
performance of a skilled task, or in the effects on learning
or performance of noise or fatigue. On the more theoretical
side, the general problems of learning, perception and
decision-making are also important, because of the interest
in producing man-made devices which will perform these
kinds of functions. Here the experimental psychologist is
likely to be working with engineers, mathematicians or computer experts on fundamental problems which will have
great practical importance in the immediate future.

In principle, the methods of experimental psychology are
similar to those of most other sciences, but there are a
number of difficulties which are more pronounced in
psychology than elsewhere. The experimental psychologist
may be collecting information about human or animal
behaviour, or he may be interested in explaining the underlying mechanisms of behaviour, using experimental methods

to test different theories. Both of these activities are complicated by the many differences which occur between individual people or animals, and by the large number of variable factors which are present in any psychological investigation and which must be taken into account. These two complications are dealt with by using the techniques of statistics, which are of great importance in nearly all branches of psychology. If, for example, you are interested in finding out the time taken by car drivers to react to a sudden stimulus, then it is not enough just to determine the average time for a number of drivers, as this tells you nothing at all about the differences between individual drivers. It is also necessary to make an estimate of the amount of variability there is between the times of different drivers, which is a measure of the extent of individual differences. Statistical methods can also help in sorting out the effects of different variable factors in an experimental situation.

Perhaps the most difficult part of experimental psychology is the attempt to explain the underlying mechanisms of behaviour. In some instances experimental observations can be explained in terms of the underlying physiology of the nervous system. For example, many of the simpler facts about perception can be explained in terms of what is known about the physiology of the sense organs and their nerve pathways to the brain. However, for most of the topics studied in experimental psychology a physiological type of explanation is not possible in the present state of knowledge. The alternative is an explanation in functional terms, where it is assumed that the brain performs certain functions, but without attempting to explain the exact mechanisms by which these are performed. A useful analogy may be made here with electronic computers. You can explain how a computer works in purely functional terms without having to understand the details of its electronic circuits, so it should similarly be possible to understand the functioning of the brain without recourse to the details of its physiology. Thus you can take specific processes or operations such as memory or speech recognition and develop theories about the way in which they work, and these theories can then be tested by experimental observation.

There are still a number of difficulties about making theories in these functional terms. For any set of experimental results in psychology there are usually a large number of possible theories which could explain them. An experiment which tends to support or reject just one theory will be of little value if there are still many other possible explanations, and part of the art of psychological research lies in devising experiments which will quickly narrow down the number of possible theories by differentiating between groups of them at a time.

A further difficulty lies in the very many different types of language or concept which have been used for constructing theories. There is as yet no really suitable language for describing fully such a highly organised and richly connected system as the brain. The terms which are used have been derived from many different sources, including physiology, physics, engineering and computer science, and the experimental psychologist must have some familiarity with the fundamental ideas of these subjects, as well as with the concepts of information theory and cybernetics, which are the sciences of communication and control systems. At present one of the most commonly used set of concepts is derived from computer terminology, as computers are the most complex mechanisms yet designed by man. Even so, the brain is vastly more complex than any computer, and different in many ways, so that this form of language is still inadequate for describing many of the functions performed by the brain.

One unique aspect of experimental psychology as a science is that while you are able to make an objective study of behaviour, you also have your own subjective experiences while engaged in this task. Thus you can study perception either by observing the behaviour of other people or by describing your own subjective experience of it. There have been disputes between different schools of psychology on this question, with some people holding that you should only study observable behaviour and others maintaining that you should concentrate on subjective impressions and experiences. On the whole, these disputes have now subsided. Psychologists now usually do study observable behaviour in their experiments, not for any dogmatic reason but because it gives much more reliable and reproducible results. The difficulty with subjective experiences is that there is no common language for talking about them, so that it is difficult to know whether two people are describing the same experience or not. However, subjective experience probably does play an important part in helping the experimental psychologist to choose successful theories. When there are so many possible theories to explain observed behaviour, a lot of intuition and insight is needed to choose the most promising one, and a theory which agrees with one's subjective experience seems more likely to be a reasonable one, although it will still be necessary to test it experimentally in terms of observed behaviour.

The activities of the brain can conveniently be divided, using computer terminology, into the four main classes shown below, and the remainder of this chapter is therefore subdivided in this way.

1. The input and preliminary processing of information, which is usually known as perception.

2. The storage of information, which covers the topics of learning and memory.

3. Central processing of information, which includes activities such as thinking, problem-solving and decision-making.

4. The output processes and the co-ordination of these with the input processes. This includes all studies of the manner in which the organism interacts with the environment and, in particular, of the highly co-ordinated activities found in any form of skilled performance.

Perception

A surprising amount can be deduced about the mechanisms of perception from very elementary observations. For example, try a very simple experiment. Look directly at an electric-light bulb (not too bright a one) for a few seconds, and then quickly move your eyes to look at a plain surface such as a wall or ceiling. Note down what you observe, and also notice what happens if you blink several times or move your hand slowly up and down in front of your eyes after the first effects have disappeared. This experiment is a good example of the difficulty of making accurate observations of your own subjective impressions. Try it on a number of different people and you will probably find a wide variety of subjective reports. If, however, you tell them what they should observe, there will probably be much more agreement, which may be partly due to the powers of persuasion but is mainly because some training is necessary in making accurate observations of this kind.

There are several effects which can be observed in this experiment. Immediately on looking at the plain surface you will probably see a bright image of the light bulb, or of its filament if it is a clear-glass bulb. After a short time this will turn into a dark image, probably of a blue-green colour. If you see several images or a blurred image, this is because your eyes have moved while looking at the light, so try again keeping your gaze fixed on the bulb for the short time that you are looking at it. The dark image will disappear fairly quickly, but can be brought back again after blinking or moving the hand across the eye, and can be made to reappear even two or three minutes after looking at the light bulb. You may notice that the bright image seems to reappear actually during the blink or while the hand is in front of the eye.

These images are called after-images, the light and dark images being called the positive and negative after-images respectively, and they can be explained fairly well in terms of what is known of the physiology of the visual system. In vision, a picture of the outside world is first formed on the retina at the back of the eye. Here the receptors, the rods and cones, contain a pigment which is sensitive to light and convert the light energy into nerve impulses. The rods and cones are connected to a complex network of nerve fibres in the retina, and these are connected to the brain by the fibres of the optic nerve. The optic nerves from the two eyes join and cross in a complex manner before they reach the visual cortex, which is the special region of the brain concerned with visual functions. Most visual observations can be explained in physiological terms involving one or more of these different stages in the process of vision.

If the above experiment is repeated, viewing the light with only one eye and observing the blank surface with the other eye, then no after-images are seen. The effects are found to occur separately for each eye, and their explanation must therefore be sought at a stage in the visual system before the optic nerves from the two eyes join together. In fact, the properties of after-images can be explained at the level of the retina. The precise details of the mechanisms involved are not all known, but in general terms the bright or positive after-image probably results from the nerves in the retina continuing to produce impulses after the stimulating light has gone. The dark or negative after-image is mainly due to the pigment in the rods and cones being bleached away by the light. The pigment takes some time to recover, so that the area which was illuminated is less sensitive for several minutes afterwards, and thus appears dark when we are looking at a plain surface. The blue-green colour of the after-image is due to the fact that pigments sensitive to different colours are present in the cones, and the light from an electric light bulb tends to bleach the red pigment more than the others so that the illuminated area is relatively more sensitive to green and blue light.

The disappearance and reappearance of the after-image has a simple physiological explanation. When light falls on the rods and cones, a burst of nerve impulses is produced when the light first appears, but this burst of impulses dies away after about one second if the light remains on. This effect is known as adaptation, and it is found at a number of different stages in the process of perception. The nervous system tends to adapt to any relatively constant stimulus conditions, and to react only to the onset of a stimulus, or any other change in the stimuli. This is biologically useful to the organism in producing a tendency to respond to

changes in the environment rather than to constant conditions. In the present example the nerves in the retina adapt
to any constant picture on the rods and cones, and will cease
to produce nerve impulses after about a second. The after-
image is effectively a fixed image on the retina, and so it is
only seen for about a second before it disappears, but an
eye-blink or anything else producing a change in illumination will start another burst of impulses and the after-image
will again be seen for a short time. If you have been following this explanation closely you might now be asking why
objects seen normally in the outside world do not also disappear after a second. In fact, they would if it were not for
the fact that the eyes are always in continuous slight motion,
even when you are trying to keep the gaze fixed on one
point, so the picture of the outside world is always moving
about over the rods and cones and a continuous stream of
nerve impulses results. With special techniques, such as
fixing a small lens and a very lightweight stimulus card to a
contact lens, the object can be made to move with the eye
so that its image is in a fixed position on the rods and
cones, and under these conditions the object does disappear
from view after a very short time.

A second simple observation gives interesting results about
another aspect of visual perception. If you can find a waterfall or a bridge over a shallow stream of water, keep your
gaze fixed for about half a minute on a rock behind the
waterfall or on a stone at the bottom of the stream, and
then look at the bank. A very curious effect is produced of
apparent movement in the opposite direction to that of the
water, but with nothing appearing to change position. This
is an after-effect of seeing movement, often known as the
waterfall effect, but it can be observed with any fairly slow
regular form of movement, provided the eyes are kept on
a fixed point and do not follow the movement itself. A very
simple demonstration of the effect can be made by looking
at the centre of a wheel, or a disc marked with radial lines,
which is slowly turning. If it is suddenly stopped after
turning for about half a minute it will appear for a short
time to move in the opposite direction. The best example

of this effect is a disc on which a black and white spiral is drawn, with the black and white in equal proportions. Rotating this one way about its centre will produce an apparent movement towards the centre during rotation, and on stopping the rotation suddenly, the spiral or anything else looked at will appear to expand outwards—looking at someone's face produces quite an alarming effect under these conditions.

This effect is another example of the principle of adaptation. Some part of the visual system must detect movement, and it seems that this mechanism adapts to any continuous movement stimulation, so that the sudden cessation of the movement is interpreted as movement in the opposite direction. Try the experiment of looking at the movement with only one eye, close this eye when the movement stops and see if the after-effect is obtained with the opposite eye. Unlike the previous experiment with after-images, the after-effect of motion is obtained when viewed with the opposite eye. This suggests, although it is not quite a conclusive argument, that the physiological mechanisms involved are at a level after the optic nerves from the two eyes join, and thus probably in the visual cortex. The detailed explanation of this effect is less certain, but physiological experiments have shown that there are nerve cells in the visual cortex which will respond to movement in a particular direction, and it is quite possible that the necessary adaptation mechanism may occur at the level of these or related cells.

The perception of movement in general is an interesting topic as there seem to be two quite separate mechanisms involved. The mechanism described above responds directly to movement across the retina when the eye remains still. However, we can also detect movement by noticing the change in the position of an object relative to its surroundings. We seem to build up a stable picture of the outside world which is, remarkably, unaffected by moving the eyes around, and any change in the position of an object in this picture is interpreted as movement. This is a complex system, the physiological details of which are not yet known, but an explanation in functional terms is quite possible, and sufficient to give us an understanding of the kind of mechanism involved. In functional terms we assume that some part of the brain is concerned with forming a stable visual picture of the outside world. This will receive information from the retina about the image falling on to the rods and cones, and it must also receive information about the movements of the eyes, so that it can make the necessary corrections for these and keep the resulting picture stable. Having achieved a stable picture, a further mechanism must then detect any changes in the position of objects in the picture, and this will be interpreted as movement.

The curious subjective experience during the after-effect of motion is connected with the fact that the two mechanisms which detect motion are giving conflicting reports. The retinal movement detector is indicating the presence of movement, because it has adapted to the continuous motion and is responding to a change in this, while the other mechanism does not detect any movement resulting from change of position. The retinal movement detector has a reasonably good physiological explanation, while the mechanism of the change of position detector can be explained at a functional level in terms of units having certain properties and the relations between them. In functional terms it is convenient to talk about a unit building up a picture of the outside world, although physiologically this 'picture' is probably represented by a complex pattern of nerve impulses which will bear no apparent resemblance to the image on the retina.

Quite a lot is now known about the physiology of the different stages of the visual system, and it is clear that the retina and optic nerves do much more than just convey the picture to the brain. Much of the analysis of the picture is actually carried out in the early stages of the visual process. If two adjacent areas of the picture on the retina receive the same amount of light, the underlying nerves in the retina will inhibit each other so that very few impulses are sent up the optic nerve to the brain. Only where there is a difference in the brightness of two adjacent areas of the picture will a large number of nerve impulses carry information to the brain. Thus if you are looking at a plain white sheet of paper lying on a table there will be inhibition over most of the retinal area covered by the image of the paper, and information will be sent to the brain only from the border of the paper where there is a difference in brightness between the paper and the table. If the table has a textured surface, such as wood, there will then be many differences between adjacent small areas, and nerve impulses will go to the brain from these regions of the retina conveying information about the texture of the surface. This general mechanism is known as lateral inhibition, and has the property of sharpening the contrast at the borders of objects. For this reason outline drawings of objects such as a human face appear so realistic, when physically there is very little similarity between an object and a drawing in terms of a comparison between the amounts of light coming from different areas.

Other physiological mechanisms in vision include nerve cells at various levels which respond only to very specific stimuli, such as lines orientated in one particular direction or movement in a given direction over a particular part of the retina, and in the visual cortex there are cells which will respond to a line orientated in a particular direction wherever it appears in the visual field. These are some of the first stages in the mechanisms of form or shape perception, and are of great interest in that they show that some of the elements of form perception are definitely built into the nervous system. The perception of forms and shapes has been studied by experimental psychologists for some time, and there is still dispute about how much shape discrimination is learned and how much is innate or built in. Many studies have been made of shape discrimination in animals, and certainly some animals, particularly birds and fish, seem to have some quite complex innate perceptual mechanisms. In mammals, on the other hand, and particularly in monkeys and human beings, learning seems to be of much greater importance, and fairly complicated discriminations can be made at quite an early age. Young children, for example, very quickly learn to discriminate between dogs and cats, not only between real animals seen from any angle but also between pictures and line drawings of them by a variety of different artists. They can hardly be judging by any one particular feature of each animal, but must be using some very complex relations between the various features. These aspects of perception are very difficult to analyse, as they are a reflection of the complexity of the brain, and of the complex nature of most stimuli in the outside world. Many experimental psychologists, understandably, restrict their studies to much simpler situations which are easier to analyse, even if of less immediate relevance to real life.

One point which is clear from studies of vision is that the process of perception consists of successive stages of analysis of the picture falling on the retina, and that a lot of processing of the information from the picture is done at quite an early stage. This does not fit in well with the older, and rather philosophical, concept of two main processes, namely sensation and perception. It used to be held that one had simple sensations such as being aware of the presence of a light, and the more complex perceptions of whole objects. However, a detailed analysis shows that no clear dividing line can be made between sensations and perceptions, and as there are many more than two stages of analysis, the concept of sensation, although attractive from a philosophical point of view, has tended to be discarded in experimental psychology.

The general principles, found in visual perception, of adaptation to constant stimulus conditions, inhibition and several stages of analysis of the sensory input are also found in perception through the other senses. The physiological details are different for each sense, and in general not so well known as for vision, and different types of complexity arise in each case. In auditory perception a very common observation can be made if you are in a room in which there is a quiet background noise such as a clock ticking. When you listen to the tick you can hear it quite clearly, but you cease to notice it if you start to read or concentrate on something else. This is not an example of adaptation because you do hear the sound for as long as you concentrate on it, but it is probably due to inhibition of the auditory nerve fibres whenever the brain is concentrating on inputs from any of the other senses. Within the ear itself is a very intricate mechanism by which different patterns of nerve impulses are produced for notes of different pitch. However, one of the facts about auditory perception is that we hear tunes as very similar whether or not they are transposed up or down a few notes, and we respond to words and phrases spoken in different voices having quite different sound frequencies. There must therefore be an important mechanism in auditory perception which analyses the relative differences between sounds independently of their absolute levels.

Another complex aspect of auditory perception is the way in which we perceive the direction and position of a source of sound. Sound takes time to travel through the air, so that unless a sound is coming from directly in front of or behind the head there will be a difference in the time at which the sound reaches the two ears. Carefully controlled experiments with very simple stimuli show that people can detect whether a sound is coming from different angles to the left or right of them according to this difference in time. In practice, however, people can usually do much better than this, and with the more complex sounds of everyday life the distance and direction of a noise can usually be detected quite well. This results from the analysis of a very complex stimulus situation. Any complex sound contains a number of different frequencies, and in an ordinary room the sounds will be reflected from a large number of different surfaces and will arrive at the ears from many different directions with slightly different time delays according to the distances the sound waves have travelled. In addition, the air tends to absorb high-frequency sounds relatively more than low-frequency ones, and if the sound is a familiar one this fact will give a cue as to the distance of the source. This is another example of a real-life situation being much more complex than most simple laboratory experiments.

Perception by means of the other senses can be equally

complex, but shows the operation of the same general principles. The sense of smell shows the property of adaptation. People living in the country and in the city adapt to the smells of manure and car-exhaust fumes respectively, but are immediately conscious of the other smell when they travel. The mechanism of temperature perception also shows adaptation, which can be demonstrated by immersing one hand in warm water and the other in cold for about a minute and then putting both hands in tepid water, which immediately feels cold to the hand which had been in warm water and warm to the other hand. This is probably due to adaptation in the temperature receptors in the skin of the hands. In touch perception, adaptation at a more complex level can be demonstrated in a simple experiment. Take two coins of different sizes, such as a sixpence and half a crown, and hold one in the tips of the fingers of each hand, with the fingers stretched out and spaced fairly equally around the circumference of the coin. After about half a minute release the coins and pick up two equal coins, such as two shillings, holding one in each hand in the same way. You will probably notice a marked difference in the apparent size of the two equal coins, even if you are actually looking at them at the time. This effect cannot be due to adaptation of the touch and pressure receptors in the skin, as these have been equally stimulated by the two different coins. It must therefore be an example of adaptation at some higher level in the organisation of touch perception.

In all the senses the general properties of adaptation, inhibition and responses to specific features of the stimulus mean that only the most important aspects of the external world are conveyed to the higher centres of the brain. In terms of computer terminology, much of the preliminary processing of the input information is performed at a peripheral level. Much of the sensory input can be said to be redundant, in that it does not provide any additional information about the outside world. Thus the edges of a plain white piece of paper provide all the necessary information about its position and shape, while the visual input from the centre of the paper provides no additional information and so is redundant. Thus some of the mechanisms of perception can be described as having the function of reducing the redundancy in the sensory input. The other perceptual mechanisms are concerned with the analysis of complex features of the external stimuli, and this can be described as 'recoding' the input information, that is, putting the essential information into a different and more useful form.

Learning and Memory

To the computer engineer the problems of learning are basically concerned with the storage and retrieval of information. In learning, the present behaviour of an organism or the output of a computer is influenced by past events, and with a computer this will involve designing a memory store which is large enough to hold all the necessary information and allows the appropriate items of information to be retrieved quickly when necessary. However, this general field is probably one where the computer analogy is not a very helpful one. To the psychologist there is an important difference between memory and learning, which is brought out in the subtle distinction in ordinary language between memorising a poem and learning a poem. Memorising a poem implies just learning the sequence of words by rote learning, while learning a poem implies a much more active process of understanding its meaning. The person who has memorised a poem may give a more accurate word-for-word rendering, while the person who has learnt a poem will usually give a meaningful version which may vary in the exact wording from the original but will be said with appropriate expression and variation in the tone of voice which can only come from understanding.

It is not unfair to say that psychologists have often not laid enough stress on this distinction between memory and learning, and many of the psychological theories of learning are basically concerned with the passive stringing together of sequences of stimuli and responses, rather than with the more active processes of organising the stimuli into a meaningful pattern and incorporating these meaningful patterns into the structure of previously learnt material. These processes are much more difficult to investigate than simple memorising, but are of much more relevance to the problems of human learning.

Some of the studies of memorising are of interest, and in particular an important distinction can be made between the mechanisms of short and long-term memory. If you look up a telephone number in the directory you can usually remember it just long enough to dial it, but it is then quickly forgotten. If you happen to be interrupted before you begin to dial the number, you immediately forget most of the number and have to look it up again. From this it appears that there must be a memory store which will hold information for a short time—in fact, for as long as the brain is concentrating on the information and not distracted by anything else. This short-term store has a limited capacity, as can be shown by the following simple experiment. Read out slowly the following sets of digits to someone, asking them to repeat each set after you have read it, and noting whether or not they are correct:

8 2 5	2 7 3	5 8 2
4 9 1 6	4 2 9 5	8 6 3 7
5 0 8 3 2	9 8 3 6 1	4 3 2 8 1
6 7 2 8 9 6	8 5 3 7 5 1	6 7 2 0 9 2
5 3 8 5 3 8 1 7	9 6 8 4 2 0 3	5 8 3 9 1 6 2
3 7 2 1 4 6 8 7	4 5 9 8 7 0 9 6	2 4 8 3 6 4 9 1
2 5 9 6 8 0 7 6 4	6 8 3 4 7 5 8 2 1	7 3 8 6 2 0 3 9 5

You will probably find that most people can repeat up to 6 digits correctly, but begin to make mistakes with 7 or 8 digits. You can estimate the 'memory span' by scoring one third of a point for each correct list, that is 1 point if all the 3-digit lists are correct and so on. Then add 2 to the total for the 1- and 2-digit lists, which are not given, and the result is a measure of the span of short-term memory.

Try a variation on the experiment using letters instead of digits, making up your own lists of random letters and being careful to avoid sequences of letters which are common in the English language. You might expect that letters would be harder to remember than digits, as there are more different possibilities, but in fact you will most likely find that the memory span is still about 6 or 7. (You may, of course, obtain quite a different result, as individual differences are quite large for this kind of experiment.) The span of short-term memory generally seems to depend on the number of items which you have to remember and not too much on the nature of these items.

Dialling a telephone number usually involves memorising at least 7 digits for a short time. This is right at the limit of memory span for most people, and mistakes frequently occur during the process of dialling. Taking the digits in pairs or larger groups can help in memorising, as each group can be treated as a single item. Telephone numbers are much easier to remember if some letters are used instead of digits, particularly if they are related to the appropriate geographical area, such as CEN for a telephone exchange in the centre of a town. The change over from telephone numbers having letters and digits to all-digit numbers is one example of a situation where the knowledge gained from experimental psychology has not been applied, and where a change has been made for the sake of engineering convenience without considering the limited capabilities of human memory. If you have a dial telephone with letters as well as digits on the dial, you can help your memory of the numbers which you often have to ring by turning the digits into letters. As there are two or three possible letters for each digit, some easily memorable groups of letters can usually be produced.

This short-term memory system is quite independent of any longer-term memory. Any stimuli which we perceive, such as words or objects, seem to be temporarily stored in the short-term memory and are either transferred to a long-term memory store or are displaced by further items coming into the short-term store, when the memory trace is lost. The short-term store apparently stores items in the order in which they are perceived, and it is difficult to retrieve the material in any other order. Try repeating the experiment with the lists of digits, but this time ask your subject to repeat the list backwards after he has heard it, that is, responding 5 2 8 to 8 2 5 and so on. You will almost certainly find that the memory span for this task is very much lower, and that subjects generally find it very difficult to do. Sometimes, after a lot of practice, people can become quite good at this task, particularly if the stimulus lists are read quite slowly, but this probably involves transferring the material to other centres in the brain, reversing the order of the items there and then sending it back to the short-term memory store. Many apparently simple experiments in psychology are complicated by the fact that some subjects can perform these kind of operations, and use parts of the brain other than the one which the experimenter thinks he is studying, and this is one of the reasons why such large individual differences are found in these kind of experiments.

In some experimental studies of memory psychologists have tried to study the rote learning of meaningless material, in an attempt to study memorising in its pure form. They have usually used lists of 'nonsense syllables', which are normally 3-letter words such as biv, xot, haj, zik, dep, hyf, lof, req, yuf, pij, ryl, qec. If you want to try a learning experiment, write these or similar syllables on separate cards and show them to a subject at a rate of about one card every 2 seconds. Then repeat the list, asking him to say each word before it is shown and score the correct responses. Continue the trials until the whole list is repeated correctly. A few generalisations may be made about the results of these studies, such as that words near the beginning and end of the list tend to be learned first, and that if two rather similar lists are learned, then words tend to become transferred from one list to the other during recall. However, even in these experiments the subjects seem to be seeking for meaning in the nonsense material, and will remember some of the syllables better than the others because they can see more meaning in them. This complicates the results of these experiments and makes it doubtful if one can ever obtain completely meaningless material.

A number of different theories of learning have been

F 69

suggested, and most of these have been concerned with the ways in which simple stimuli are linked to simple responses. Some of these theories are based on the concept of conditioning, which derives from the work of the Russian psychologist, Pavlov. Dogs will normally salivate at the sight of food, which is a simple response to a relatively simple stimulus, and the amount of saliva in the mouth gives a measure of the intensity of the response. Pavlov trained his dogs by ringing a bell just before the food was presented, and found that the dogs would salivate on hearing the bell. He called this the conditioned (or conditional) response. Thus learning by conditioning essentially consists of linking a response to a new stimulus.

Other theories of learning have extended this basic idea of forming links between stimuli and responses, and have produced models describing how the strengths of these links are related to variables such as drive or incentive. These models or theories are functional explanations, and the variables are assumed to be internal states of the organism related to the observed behaviour which can be measured. The majority of the models have been applied to animal behaviour, particularly that of rats running through mazes, which is a convenient, if somewhat artificial, situation for experimental study.

There are many possible theoretical models of this type which can be suggested, and thousands of rats have run through mazes in psychological laboratories in order to settle disputes between rival theories. However, one criticism of all these theories is their assumption that a particular response is transferred from one stimulus to another. In fact, the conditioned response is often rather different from the normal response, and dogs salivating to the sound of a bell produce considerably less saliva than when the food is actually presented. Also, the exact nature of the response is not always important. In one experiment rats were taught to run through a maze, and thus could be assumed to have built up connexions between the stimuli of the maze and the motor responses of running. The maze was then filled with water and the rats managed successfully to swim through the correct route, although the motor responses they were making were quite different. A better type of theoretical model would thus assume that it is sequences of stimuli which are learnt, and that the appropriate responses are made to reach the next stimulus. Theories of this type have had some success in explaining experimental results, but have still tended not to be concerned with the problems of responding to complex stimuli.

One approach which does emphasise the organising of stimuli into meaningful patterns stems from the studies of memory by the British psychologist, Bartlett. He employed the idea of a schema (borrowed from the work of the neurologist, Henry Head). This he supposed to be an organised structure, which is gradually built up during the process of learning. People brought up in different ways or in different cultures will tend to differ in their schematic models of their environment, which may affect the way in which they perceive and react to it. Bartlett found that many of the errors in the remembering of material are caused by mistakes in its original perception. He considered perception as being influenced by the schema, and that material which did not fit into the schematic model may be ignored or perceived and remembered in a distorted form.

This idea of learning as essentially a process of building up schemata is basically similar to the building up of concepts in many forms of human learning. The study of this has particular relevance to the teaching of subjects like mathematics, where it is essential to understand one concept before going on to others which are built on its foundation.

Apart from the studies of conceptual and schematic learning, many of the psychological studies of learning are not of very direct relevance to actual human learning. A few general principles are, however, worth mentioning, as they have been found in a wide variety of studies. For any one type of material it is generally best to space the sessions of learning over a period of time rather than to run them consecutively. It is also not advisable to study two similar types of material in successive sessions or interference may result between the two. This is the principle which governs the planning of school and college timetables, where the different subjects are spread out over the day, and ideally subjects such as French and German should not be studied one immediately after the other. Another general principle is that mistakes in the initial learning of material are very hard to eradicate. If you make a mistake in translating a French word the first time you meet it, you will often find yourself repeating the same mistake on later occasions, even though you have been corrected several times. Many of the traditional methods of schoolteaching, and university and college lecturing, do not overcome this problem. Often in mathematics a pupil may make a mistake in the method of making a calculation, and may have done a whole page of incorrect examples before this is noticed by the teacher. He will then have built up a very strong set of incorrect responses which is difficult to alter.

Ideally one requires a teaching situation in which the learner is guided into making the correct response, and where he is immediately made aware of any mistake. Apart from individual tuition, one way in which this has been attempted is by the techniques of programmed learning. In this, material is prepared rather as in a book, but with gaps every so often where the reader has to fill in the missing words or figures. The correct answer is printed in such a way that it is not visible while the question is being answered but can be seen immediately afterwards. (The simplest way of achieving this is by printing the answers over on the right-hand side of a page, and covering them with a piece of paper which is moved down to reveal each answer as appropriate.) By suitably choosing the places where responses are called for, the learner can be guided into thinking in the right way so that he will usually make the correct response, and any errors are immediately seen. The material can either be presented in book form or by using a teaching machine. The machine mainly acts as a mechanical device to present the material and prevent cheating, and can also enable extra teaching material to be provided when mistakes are made, but in general it has little advantage over book presentation. The more important point concerning programmed learning is the way in which the material is prepared. Some programmes have been based on the simpler theories of learning and emphasise the making of the correct responses, often in a very repetitive way, while other programmes have been written with the intention of building up concepts and are more concerned with producing the right way of thinking about the problems.

Central Processes and Skilled Performance

The more central processes of the brain are difficult to study directly, and generally one can only make deductions about the nature of these processes by observing the behaviour related to them. Activities such as thinking probably involve the co-ordinated functioning of very many different areas of the brain, and normal physiological studies are not very helpful as they usually involve the detailed functioning of only one area. Explanations at a functional level are therefore necessary, and some quite useful general analogies arise with the operation and programming of electronic computers, although here again the analogy must not be followed too closely.

The way in which a computer functions when it is solving a problem is determined by a programme, which essentially consists of instructions for transferring information from one section to another and for performing certain simple operations. The set of instructions used is called the 'language' in which the programme is written, and several possible languages may be used. The 'machine language' is the set of detailed basic instructions which will perform the individual steps of the various operations. This language is usually quite complicated, and is unique to any particular model of computer. Even performing a simple operation such as adding two numbers may require a large number of these detailed instructions, so the programme in the machine language will tend to be rather long and cumbersome. Another language is therefore used, in which each instruction may represent a number of these basic machine instructions. This is usually called a 'higher level language', and instructions in this language are translated into the basic instructions of the machine language by a special part of the computer known as a compiler. Programmes are much easier to write in a higher level language, and in addition the same language can be used for many different computers, as each can have its own compiler for translating into the detailed instructions of its particular machine language.

This seems to provide a useful model for discussing the nature of the central processes which occur during thinking, although in the human brain one can imagine several different levels of language, with different compilers to translate instructions from one level to another. The basic level, or machine language, would control the pattern of nerve impulses in different parts of the brain. An intermediate level language may be assumed to translate instructions into the machine language, and various forms of higher level language may convert instructions into this intermediate level language or from one higher level language to another. The machine language, and possibly the intermediate level language may be assumed to be innately determined, while the higher level languages and the compilers which translate from them to other languages may be assumed to be built up during the process of learning. Other types of model for discussing thinking are also possible, but this particular model is valuable in stressing the complexity of the processes involved and the importance of considering activities at a number of different levels.

Very marked individual differences are found in the ways in which different people think or solve problems, and these are not all due to different methods of teaching. One could say that individuals differ in the type of programme or type of language which they are using to carry out these tasks. Some interesting results concerning these individual differences can be derived from studies of subjective experiences during processes such as thinking. Some people while thinking tend to have strong visual imagery, that is they tend to see pictures or symbols, while others seem to think mainly in words, and many people report no such impressions at all—although they are usually just as good at solving problems. These types of mental imagery were first studied scientifically by the British scientist Sir Francis Galton, who had a very wide range of interests, and who himself hoped that the results might show the essential differences between the mental operations of different men. People who do not have any mental imagery often find it difficult to believe that others do, and it is interesting to ask a group of people whether they tend to think in terms of words or pictures or in 'imageless' fashion, and how clearly they can imagine pictures of past events or have 'images' in other sensory modes such as particular sounds or odours. Occasionally, people may have strong visual imagery associated with numbers or dates, sometimes seeing each one at a particular position in space or of a certain colour. Use can be made of visual imagery in a technique for improving memory, where a person is trained to associate the objects or words he has to remember with particular points in space or parts of a visualised picture. This technique is, of course, only useful to those people who have clear visual imagery.

During thinking, problem-solving and similar activities, the brain can be considered to set up a model of the external world and to carry out operations on this model. Thus predicting the outcome of different courses of action, which is one of the activities involved in thinking, can be assumed to be done by performing the appropriate operations on the model. The accuracy of these predictions will depend on how well the model represents the external world, and how accurately the operations can be carried out. Many different ways of constructing such models are possible, and the study of mental imagery may give an idea as to the nature of some of them. In terms of the computer analogy, these models can be assumed to be constructed in a higher level language. The objects in the external world and the relations between them will have a functual relation to the symbols and operations in this programming language. In people with visual imagery the model is probably structured in a very similar way to the perceived visual world, while in those people who have very little imagery the model may be constructed in quite a different way. One might expect from this that anyone with strong visual imagery would not be good at dealing with abstract problems, since they would presumably do their thinking mainly in terms of the visual world. There is some evidence for this, and Galton himself found that visual imagery was not so common among scientists, who often have to think in abstract terms.

Many central processes are not carried out in isolation but as part of a general interaction with the environment, that is, they occur as a result of external stimuli and produce responses which may affect the environment. To the psychologist these types of activity can be classed under the general heading of skilled performance. Skill is here used in a very wide sense, including some purely mental activities as well as those with some physical or muscular component. However, the general principles in all these cases are basically similar, and it is quite convenient to talk about mental skills such as speaking a foreign language, as well as the more physical skills such as operating a lathe. Skills will involve both perceptual and muscular activity, and they can be classified as mainly perceptual or motor skills according to the relative amounts of these components.

In performing a skilled task, such as driving a car, the environment will be continually changing partly because of external factors and partly because of the responses made by the driver. Here the environment includes both the road and traffic, and the controls, dials and engine of the car. Changes in the traffic conditions and in the direction of the road are constantly occurring, and the responses made to these will cause changes in the speed of the engine and the position of the car on the road. While making these responses, their resultant effects are continually observed, and these in turn modify the precise movements which are made in producing the responses. There is thus a continuous process in which a carefully controlled response is produced by observing its effects while it is being made.

This kind of behaviour can be described by the concepts

of cybernetics, which is the general science of control systems, both engineering systems and biological ones. An important idea is that of the flow of information. In a simple reaction to a stimulus, information from the stimulus can be said to flow via the senses and the brain to the muscles producing the response. In a control system in which errors are continually corrected, such as in keeping a car on its correct course, one can again say that information about the error in the position of the car flows through the senses and the brain to produce a response. This response will be in a direction so as to reduce the error, and information about the change in the error is then fed back to the senses, and in turn produces a change in the response. There is thus a continuous loop along which information flows, through the senses to the brain, to the muscles to produce a response, and then it is fed back to the senses, and so on. This feedback of information is a very important principle in control theory, and there are several relevant factors which can be studied, such as how much information can be transmitted, and how accurately, and how long it takes for information to travel around the loop. There are delays both in the brain, in the time taken to react to a stimulus, and in the time taken for the car to change its position, or similar changes in other types of mechanism, once a correcting response has been made.

These kinds of considerations show that the industrial designer must be well informed about human performance and capabilities, so that the nature and design of controls and dials in a car, a plane cockpit or on industrial equipment can be made to suit both the human capabilities of the operator and the engineering capabilities of the machine. This general field is known as systems engineering or ergonomics (a Greek form of 'work study'), and includes the study of any combined system involving both man and his physical environment. This might include a bricklayer using a trowel, a man working at a lathe, a controller in an automated factory or an aircraft pilot coming in to land, where there would be a very complex system of information flow between the pilot and the various ground controllers. With the advent of automation there has been a general trend away from motor skills involving a large amount of physical effort to perceptual skills which mainly involve the intake of a large amount of information.

One of the many practical problems in the study of skills is the effect on skilled performance of various factors in the environment, such as noise, lighting and temperature, and the effects of fatigue. Those skills, having a relatively high perceptual component, seem to be more affected by noise, and are also quite susceptible to fatigue. Fatigue is used here not in the sense of general tiredness, but to refer to the effects resulting from performing a particular skilled task for a long time. Perceptual or mental fatigue often occurs, and reduces the efficiency of performance even though there may be no physical fatigue or tiredness present. This kind of fatigue can occur very quickly in some highly perceptual skills. Many industrial inspection tasks, such as looking for small flaws in electric-light bulbs moving along a factory conveyor belt, can only be carried out efficiently for about half an hour before the performance drops off quite markedly.

This whole field is being rapidly developed, as the importance of applied experimental psychology is becoming realised. Both in industry and in research laboratories experimental psychologists now work with engineers, industrial designers and other scientists on the practical problems which arise when men perform many different kinds of skilled task, and on the more basic fundamental problems of human behaviour. This combined effort is bound to be of great practical value.

Suggested Reading

BROADBENT, D. E., *Behaviour*, London: Methuen (University Paperback), 1964.

GALTON, F., *Inquiries into Human Faculty and its Development*, London: Macmillan, 1883 (also Dent: Everyman Library).

GEORGE, F., *Cybernetics and Biology*, Edinburgh: Oliver & Boyd, 1966.

GREGORY, R. L., *Eye and Brain*, London: Weidenfeld & Nicolson, 1966.

MUELLER, C. G., *Sensory Psychology*, New York: Prentice-Hall, 1965.

Also some of the following two series of booklets are relevant to industrial psychology.

Problems of Progress in Industry, obtainable from Her Majesty's Stationery Office.

Ergonomics for Industry, obtainable from the Ministry of Technology, Warren Spring Laboratory, Stevenage, Herts.

4

Developmental Psychology

Richard R. Skemp

Developmental Processes in Man and Animal

To what extent is the development of an individual human, from birth to maturity, the realisation of a pattern determined at the moment of conception by the genetic blueprint derived from the parental germ cells? And to what extent is it determined, or influenced, by environment? This question is one which has been the subject of controversy down the ages, and it still is.

The social and political implications are far-reaching. If, for example, intelligence is mainly determined by heredity, and remains unchanged throughout the lifetime of an individual, then those capable of benefiting from higher education can be identified and selected at an early age. But if all children have equal potentiality, then by suitable education any child can be fitted for any future career. Both these views have been advanced by well-known psychologists, and might appear at first sight to have had much influence on the educational systems of their time and country. It is open to question, however, which way the influence has acted, since politicians and administrators are very capable of selecting, from a range of contemporary scientific opinion, that view which best justifies the course of action which they have already chosen on other grounds. The remedy for this is, of course, a greater awareness of the current scientific knowledge by the public at large.

Clearly, the relative influences of heredity and environment will be different according to which physical, behavioural or mental characteristics we are interested in. If we want to know why someone speaks French or English, plays cricket or baseball, wears his hair long or crew-cut, we shall expect to find the causes in his environment. But if, probing deeper, we ask why he is capable of learning to speak at all, in any language, then the basic requirement is the possession of sufficiently high intelligence. Other animal species have adequate vocal apparatus, and so do very subnormal children, but by no environmental influences can they be enabled to speak. We can play ball games because of our erect posture and prehensile hands—both hereditary traits. And the (natural) colour of the hair, however styled, is another hereditary characteristic. The development of an individual person can therefore only be properly understood in terms of the interaction of heredity and environment, with different weights on each according to which aspect of him (or her) we are considering.

But how are these underlying hereditary characteristics themselves determined? Immediately, of course, by those of the parents; who derive them from their parents, and so on backwards in time. We see that even partly to understand the development, during his lifetime, of an individual man, we must look farther back still and consider the evolution of the species 'man', and the process of natural selection by which his hereditary characteristics have been determined: not only the more obvious physical characteristics but also the mental abilities which most distinguish man from all the other animal species.

Most readers will have some acquaintance with the basic theory, propounded by Charles Darwin in *The Origin of Species*. Briefly, its main points are:

(i) Species perpetuate themselves by reproduction of their own kind.

(ii) Not all these offspring can survive to maturity.

(iii) Certain characteristics may increase the probability of survival to maturity of individuals which have these characteristics;

(iv) and hence, in turn, of their reproducing.

(v) These individuals will therefore contribute a some-what larger proportion to the next generation.

(vi) If (and only if) these survival-producing characteristics are hereditary, they will appear in a greater proportion of each successive generation;

(vii) and will thus become established in the species by a process of 'natural selection'.

The characteristics of a species, both physical and mental, are thus very closely related to its survival. But 'survival' is not an absolute term—it means 'survival in a given environment'. Change the environment, and the survival value of a particular characteristic is likely to change too: possibly for the better, usually for the worse. For example, the stripes of a zebra are valuable camouflage in its native habitat: but would make it highly conspicuous in open country. To the extent that these characteristics are firmly fixed by heredity, an individual will be unable to adapt for survival in a different environment. And since the physical surroundings are constantly changing over most of the earth's surface, *adaptability*—the ability to develop new survival characteristics for new circumstances—will itself have survival value, and we should expect at least some species to evolve having this quality.

Of all animals, man is the most adaptable. No other single species can live at the tropics, in polar regions, on the surface of the sea, deep beneath it and high in the stratosphere. What is the secret of his adaptability?

Not in any of his physical abilities. Name any of these—vision, hearing, running, strength, ability, endurance—and it is easy to name other species which surpass him. It is in the organisation of his behaviour, and, above all, on the capacity to learn, during his lifetime, new ways of organising his behaviour, that man excels.

Adaptive behaviour is, after all, even more important for survival than physical characteristics. For example, keen scent, all-round vision and powerful running muscles are of no value to a deer unless these are suitably employed to give information of the approach of a predator, and to make escape easier in good time. Complementary to adaptive physical characteristics, we therefore find adaptive behaviour patterns, which may be innate, learnt, or innate but modified by learning.

Some animals are born physically capable of survival behaviour patterns. The baby crocodile hatches from its egg in the hot sun by the banks of the Nile with all the behaviour patterns necessary to look after itself, and in due course to reproduce its species. It never sees its parents, nor does it need to. Others, such as kittens, piglets, chickens and goslings, and baby thrushes, are born physically incapable of independent survival, and are nurtured by their parents until such time as they become so capable. The innate behaviour patterns which appear first are such as enable the young to make use of, and indeed to evoke, the nurturing behaviour of their parents. Kittens and piglets are born with a knowledge of how to suck. Chicks can peck corn, and will run to the sound of a mother hen's clucking. Baby thrushes will tilt their heads back, and open their beaks, when a mother thrush appears overhead.

These innate behaviour patterns have two major limitations. They are predetermined by heredity, not developed in relation to the actual environment: i.e. they are preadapted, not adaptable. And they are responses to stimuli representing only a very small part of the appropriate object. Chicks will run to a tape-recorder which is playing back a record of a mother hen's clucking. Baby thrushes will gape with their beaks at a finger held overhead. Greylag goslings will follow a distinguished professor if he imitates the sound of a Greylag goose. These assorted objects each resemble the nurturing parents only in one particular way, but the young respond to them as if they were, in fact, mother hen, thrush or goose.

This becomes understandable if we consider the tiny size of the chromosomes within the nuclei of the germ cells. These contain the genetic information necessary to determine not only the whole of the physical characteristics but also all the innate behaviour patterns of the individual. It is an astonishing piece of miniaturisation—as though the blue-print of a television receiver were able to determine not only the circuit but the ability of the set when constructed to discriminate between, say, Bach and the Beatles, and to respond appropriately. This could only be done by isolating a simple but characteristic part of the respective incoming signals, and designing filter circuits to discriminate between these. The receiver would not really be responding to Bach or the Beatles, as such, and could easily be deceived if (say) a Bach programme were introduced by a vigorous tattoo on the drums. In the same way, there is a limit to the complexity of the behaviour which can be transmitted genetically. Sucking, but not speech; mating, but not mathematics.

This genetic bottleneck can, however, be by-passed by a species which has evolved the ability to learn: which is to say, above all, by man. Born not only physically helpless but with a minimal set of innate survival behaviours, the learning capacity of the young is now limited not by what can be coded on to a score or so of complex protein molecules but by the total storage capacity of the central nervous system, with its millions of nerve cells and interconnexions. It is like the difference in purchasing power between a child's money-box and the vaults of Fort Knox. The resemblance may be taken a step farther, since it is the present writer's belief that the potential ability of the human mind is still largely unused.

This, moreover, brings an unexpected bonus, in that the accumulated knowledge of previous generations now becomes available to each new generation. A new survival behaviour—making a bow and arrow, a jet engine—may be the life work of a highly gifted individual. Yet these techniques can be learnt in a relatively short time by all who follow. The developing human learns partly from his own experience, but vastly more from the total experience of his species—stored no longer in the germ cells of his parents but in their brains, in the brains of his teachers at school and after, and above all in the books, microfilms, tapes and other forms of stored symbolic information.

The ability to store knowledge outside himself in the form

of symbols represents a difference in kind, and not just in degree, between the learning abilities of man and of other species. Many other animals can learn, in varying degrees: none but man can learn to read and write.

Man thus represents a breakthrough in evolution, mainly on the strength of this one quality—a greatly superior ability to learn. Much else might be said in elaboration of this point, but space must limit us here to two.

First: this ability has a direct physiological basis, namely, our much larger and more convoluted cerebral cortex. And this physiological characteristic has been evolved by natural selection, and is transmitted genetically. Our ability to by-pass the genetic storage of survival behaviour is, nevertheless, genetically transmitted. Instead of being born with a small number of relatively simple in-born behaviours, we are born with the physiological basis of the ability to acquire a much greater number of vastly more complex behaviours.

Second: the chief price we pay for this is a much longer period of nurture during which we are relatively helpless to survive unaided, while we learn how to look after ourselves first of all physically, and then socially and economically.

Maturation, learning and imprinting

Our study of human development began a long way back, for two reasons. First, because the unique abilities of man can best be seen by comparing him with other species. Second, because it is not only those qualities of the individual which are determined at the moment of conception (such as sex, hair colour) but also those which enable him to learn adaptive behaviour after birth (such as intelligence, curiosity), which are genetically determined. Not only the fixed characteristics (such as erect posture, binocular vision) but also the ability to vary one's behaviour according to a changing environment, are the product of millions of years of evolution by natural selection, and they cannot be adequately understood except in relation to this context.

In this section, we shall begin to consider these two factors—innate characteristics, and those learnt by interaction with the environment—as they may be seen in operation during the development of a child from birth to maturity.

So far as behaviour is concerned, as opposed to physical qualities, the effects of these two factors can seldom be seen in isolation. Even the simplest innate behaviours of man are mostly, to some extent, modified by learning. We learn to control even, such basic and innate responses as coughing, or dropping something hot. And even the most complex learnt activities have as their starting-point, if we trace them back far enough, some innate behaviour or response tendency: nothing starts quite from nothing. Reading, for example, is dependent on central fixation by the eye. This is initially reflex, but we gradually learn to control it. Another complication arises from the fact that parents not only give a child his genetic constitution but are usually the most influential part of his early environment. If a child resembles his parents in character and behaviour, how much of this is hereditary and how much environmental?

Two further difficulties arise from the fact that some kinds of instinctual behaviour, and also some kinds of learning, only take place at certain times. Nest building is innate in birds, but does not show itself until they are sexually mature, and then only at certain seasons and at certain stages in the sequence: courtship—mating—raising of the young. The delayed appearance of innate characteristics is called *maturation*. In distinction to this, the tendency to choose other members of their own species as mates appears, surprisingly, not always to be innate, but learnt at certain critical periods in the life of the individual. This phenomenon, called *imprinting*, will be discussed further in the next section.

Perhaps the greatest difficulty of all is that of experimenting with human beings. How do we know that a particular behaviour pattern is innate in a certain animal? One way is to deprive an individual of opportunities for learning it, and see whether the behaviour still appears. This may involve physical restraint, or isolation from other members of the species. Pigeons reared in glass tubes which prevented them from flapping their wings were, when released, able to fly at the same age as others from the same clutch of eggs. The song of chaffinches reared in isolation resembled in some respects, but not all, the song of those raised in contact with others of their species, indicating that in this case the song-pattern was partly innate and partly learnt. But we cannot usually do this kind of experiment with human children, for ethical reasons. Occasionally, accident or social custom provides us with a ready-made experiment. Feral children (children lost by their parents and said to be raised by wild animals) are occasionally found. Observation of these children indicates that human speech is learnt, not innate. In a study of children of the Hopi Indians, it was found that those infants who were bound to a cradleboard continuously for the first three months of life, and intermittently thereafter till about fourteen months of age, showed no difference in the age of walking from those without cradleboards. This, and a number of other such studies, support the view that crawling and walking are innate, and appear as a result of maturation and not of learning.

The two experimental conditions which we would like, ideally, are: first, two children of identical genetic constitution, raised under different environmental conditions. Differences which appeared between these would be ascribable to learning. Second, two children of different genetic constitution, raised under identical conditions. Differences between these could then be ascribed to heredity.

Of these, the first is not too difficult to achieve: the second is almost impossible. Different families treat their children in different ways. Within the same family, parents apply to the younger children experience gained with the older ones. Moreover, the position of a child relative to brothers and sisters is a most important factor of the social environment of a child, as is being clearly shown by a large-scale current survey of British children. Even if we take dissimilar twins, each of these is a very important part of the environment of the other: so they would have to be raised separately from each other, but otherwise in the same way by the same parents.

Identical twins, however, are not infrequent. Occasionally

they are separated early in life (e.g. adopted by different parents), and if they can be traced, these pairs can provide much interesting information. More often they are raised together, and it is then possible, if their parents are experimental psychologists (or willing for other reasons to take part in such a study), to give them different experiences within particular areas of development, against backgrounds which are broadly similar in other respects. This can be done well within the limits of what, by omission or commission, might adversely affect the child's development.

One famous study* of this kind is described in *Growth: A Study of Johnny and Jimmy* (see reading list). Jimmy received no special training, and was not even allowed access to stairs. Johnny was given a thorough training in various motor skills from three weeks onwards. When Johnny could climb stairs well, Jimmy was allowed to try: and within a couple of days, he could climb as well as Johnny. Climbing, therefore, would seem to be instinctive: as any parent who sees his child react to a climbing frame, seen for the first time, will find it easy to believe. But in certain other respects, such as roller skating, Johnny (who received special training) remained far ahead of his twin. We conclude that this ability is not innate in human beings!

Toilet training is an important area of early learning, so let us look at a twin study relating to this. Training of Hugh began at the age of thirty days, and he was 100 per cent 'reliable' at two years two months. Training of his twin brother Hilton began at two years, and he reached the same degree of reliability in two months.

This suggests that whether or not bladder control is entirely innate—both twins had some training, though Hilton had enormously less—there is a stage of maturation before which attempts to bring about learning are mostly wasted effort. This state of readiness may be reached at different ages by different children, and these individual differences may well be innate.

---

* Unfortunately, it was later discovered that these were fraternal twins, not identical. But the interest created by this study stimulated its subsequent replication with identical twins.

The idea of 'readiness' has been applied to other areas of learning, such as reading. Here, however, the evidence is less conclusive.

The learnt behaviours described above have been quoted largely by way of examples of research methods. Psychology is the scientific study of mental processes and behaviour, and it is well to see some of the problems of applying it to the complexities of human development.

But, of course, the field of learnt behaviour is vast, particularly in the early years. By the age of seven a child has learnt to understand speech, to talk, perhaps to sing; it can read a little, write a little, turn on the television receiver with great facility; it can control its elimination, dress and undress itself, turn on lights and taps, open doors, control a tricycle very skilfully and perhaps also a bicycle. This list above could be continued almost indefinitely. Parallel with this is social learning: to live in co-operation with the rest of its family, to obey most of the requests of its parents, to conform to some of their wishes even in their absence; and to play, amicably for the most part, with other children. Once we leave the field of simple physiological self-regulation (such as breathing faster after exertion), almost all the skills required for everyday life in the contemporary physical and social environment are learnt. It is clearly impossible to discuss these in detail. Instead, let us look at a few of the general principles which can be distinguished.

One of the most important of these is that the term 'learning' covers a wide spectrum of adaptive changes resulting from experience. When Pavlov's famous experiments on the conditioned reflex were published, some psychologists thought that it would be possible to account for all human learning in terms of 'conditioning'. Even today, there are still some who hold to this view: though how it is possible to explain, say, the discovery of penicillin or the invention of a radio telescope or a jet engine on this basis is hard to comprehend. There is no space here for a discussion of learning theory, but it seems important to distinguish between the more primitive forms of learning which we share with other species, such as avoiding objects (e.g. nettles) which have hurt us, from those peculiar to man such as learning to speak, read and write.

These last three related activities embody some other principles of importance. One is that of learning which makes possible other learning. Speech makes possible reading and writing, which in turn open the door to the stored knowledge of mankind. In many other areas too, one's existing knowledge and skills are essential tools for the acquisition of new knowledge.

Speech, reading and writing are also symbols whereby knowledge can pass from one individual to another without any other form of demonstration. And by the use of these and other symbols, we can try out in advance alternative sequences of actions, and pick the best before ever doing one of them. Trial and error learning by actions with real, possibly disastrous, consequences is replaced by learning *before the actual event*. This is a more difficult form of learning—it is easier to be wise after the event—but where it can be achieved, the gain in survival value is considerable. Learning to learn this way is an important feature of our development.

What does a word, or other symbol, stand for? Seldom for a single object, action or other sensory experience: almost always for a class of these, or even a relation between classes. A word stands for a concept, which may be described as an awareness of something in common between a certain set of experiences. It is this conceptual ability by which we recognise that new experiences have something in common with certain categories of past ones (a bus is a kind of motor vehicle). This will be discussed again in relation to intelligence, but the point to be made here is that the relation between words and concepts is a two-way one. Not only is the attachment of a word the result of having formed a concept: it also helps us to recognise future examples of it more easily if they have the same word attached.

Some learning is deliberate on the part of the child (e.g. learning to swim, ride a bicycle, play an instrument). Some learning is the result, voluntary or otherwise, of a deliberate activity by someone else, called teaching. But a great deal of learning appears to take place unconsciously and involuntarily. Is this really so? Or is all learning consciously motivated in some way?

This is another question too complicated to be answered here. Certainly a strong motivation may greatly increase the rate of learning: but psychologists have sometimes taken too restricted a view of the nature of motivation. This has arisen partly from the frequent use of lower animals, such as rats and pigeons, for learning experiments. These are left unfed for a while beforehand, and are rewarded with morsels of food after each performance of a certain action: which is rapidly learnt under these conditions. But most of the kind of learning which interests us in human beings takes place when we are neither hungry, thirsty, nor in any other physiological state of need. Experiments with monkeys have shown that curiosity is, in them, a very strong motivation; and few parents will resist the suggestion that this is also true for children of all ages.

But what is curiosity if not a desire to know? So to say that curiosity is a motivation is to say that, at least in man and other primates, at least some learning is self-motivating. We learn because it is in our nature to do so. Paradoxically, this pursuit of knowledge for its own sake has the greatest adaptive value of all, by virtue of the increased knowledge of the environment which it gives. And this is true whether we are talking about the exploration by a crawling child of everything he can reach, or advanced research by a scientist. The tragedy is that in so many, at some stage of their growth, this particularly human urge seems to have been extinguished.

Emotional and Social Development

Though we know what we mean by it, 'emotion' is not an easy word to define. Most would agree that it is a kind of feeling: so what kinds of feeling would we call emotions, and which not? Hunger, pain, fear, anger, love: of these, the last three would usually be described as emotions, the first two as simple physiological sensations. What all five have in common is that they produce a tendency—one might even say that they *were* a tendency—to certain kinds of behaviour. In the first two cases, the class of associated behaviours is much smaller and more specific. A hungry person tends to eat, and that is that. An angry person may hit, or utter scathing words, or write a letter to *The Times*, or start a Society for the Abolition of X. So a characteristic of an emotion is that while it may still be a powerful drive towards action, the variety of the actions which it can motivate is much greater.

We would therefore expect learning to play an important part in building up a person's repertoire of behaviour associated with a particular emotion, and this is the case. All human societies impose restraints on the ways in which individuals may acceptably express their emotions, though the details vary from one group to another. In our culture, aggression and sex are examples; and one of the things a growing child has to learn is which ways he may use to express these, and which not. Parents mediate these social requirements to a child—they reward and punish the same behaviours as will be rewarded and punished by the wider social group, but more gently. So they protect a child in two ways: by substituting smaller harms for unadaptive behaviour—reproof for neglect of kerb-drill, and praise for practising it, instead of death or maiming; and by teaching him behaviour which will enable him subsequently to fit in with the wider society. Schools have a similar task—the social education which they give is at least as important as the academic.

Less obvious, but complementary to learnt behaviour, are learnt needs. When his tricycle was stolen, my small son was greatly distressed until we bought him another. From riding one, going for tricycle trips with his playmates, and also because all his friends had them, we recognised that a tricycle had become a very real need in his life. One might well say that it was not a luxury but a necessity! Had he never owned one, nor seen and ridden those of his friends, he would not have acquired this need. Many learnt needs relate to a more basic need, to 'belong', and take the form of 'needing' clothes and possessions like those of the other members of one's group: and this was a factor, though not the only one, of the need for a tricycle.

One's feelings towards other people are also emotions. These may be temporary, or chronic, and in the latter case we call them attitudes. Like other emotions, they correspond to a tendency to certain kinds of behaviour. A friendly attitude predisposes to co-operation, proximity, generosity; a respectful attitude towards obedience, co-operation; an aggressive attitude towards rudeness, injury. We may feel them towards individuals, or towards classes of individuals; and like other emotions, these attitudes are almost entirely learnt.

The ways in which childhood experiences influence future attitudes and personal relationships may be straightforward, but often hidden factors are also at work. White American children, especially in the Southern states, rapidly acquire their parents' negative attitude towards Negroes. At a four-week camp where white and Negro boys lived and played together, away from parental influence, it was found that some white children became more tolerant towards Negroes. Others, however, became more prejudiced. Personality tests indicated that the latter had strong aggressive feelings which they had no way of expressing, that they felt the world to be hostile to them, and other people to be trying to victimise them. Given a convenient target for their aggression, they took advantage of it. Their attitudes towards Negroes were thus largely an expression of their feelings about the world in general, and ultimately, almost certainly, a result of their own parents' behaviour towards them.

Parents are the most important part of a child's early environment, and there is wide agreement among psychologists that relationships with them are major factors of attitudes and relationships in later life. This is multipliply determined. As Anna Freud has pointed out, children arrive at kindergarten or nursery school with an already well-formed set of attitudes towards, and expectations from, authority in the form of teachers. Though these are derived

94

from earlier relationships with parents, there is a tendency towards self-perpetuation. The open, friendly child tends to evoke similar attitudes from those with whom he is in later contact, and vice versa. Further, a child's opinion of himself is derived from the opinions he perceives his parents to have of him: and these, too, affect his expectations from others, peers as well as teachers. Again, there is a tendency to evoke the expected attitudes.

At a deeper level, there is much evidence that the capacity to love, in adult life, is greatly dependent on having been loved as a child; and especially on a good relationship with the mother during the first few years. Particular emphasis is placed by the psychoanalytic school of thought on early experiences connected with feeding. The baby who feels hungry, cries, is picked up, and fed, learns early that the world is basically a safe place where people help, needs are fulfilled. It is not only the food itself which seems to be important but the stimulation of being lifted, being talked to, and bodily contact. Numerous studies of infants in orphanages indicate that without the latter, adequately nourished children may fail to thrive physically, as well as showing many signs of emotional disturbance. Similar effects are found in young children separated from their mothers, e.g. by being taken to hospital. A typical sequence of behaviour in such a case is first, great distress; second, apathy, when the child ceases to give trouble and may therefore be described as having 'settled down'. On visiting day, the arrival of the mother may result in the child reverting to stage one, which is probably a step in the right direction— the distress is being expressed, not repressed. Hospital authorities may, however, consider that the parents' visit has upset the child, and regard this is an argument against visiting at all. A third typical behaviour, after separation, is rejection of the mother by the child.

A notable contribution towards informing public opinion about the effects of separation has been the work of Dr. John Bowlby (see reading list), and today a number of hospitals admit the mothers of young children to live in, take over some of the routine care of the child, and be present at critical moments such as coming round from an anaesthetic. Though this creates practical problems, not only in the hospital but also at home if there are other children, the value of this arrangement for the long-term good of the child is probably immeasurable.

Some critics of Bowlby's work have pointed out that ill effects are not an invariable result of separation. That there are individual differences in reactions to this is suggested by some animal experiments at Cambridge, by Hinde. Four young monkeys, thirty days old, were separated from their mothers for six days. In this case it was the mothers who were taken elsewhere, the baby monkeys being left in the same enclosure with the same other adult monkeys—parents, and other females. This was to isolate the factor of maternal deprivation from that of removal to a strange new environment, which is also present for children taken to hospital. All the baby monkeys, and their mothers, showed great distress for the whole of the period of separation. When they were together again, all the babies spent much more time clinging to their mothers for the first few days. For two of the four babies, this wore off within a few weeks. But the other two were still over-clinging a year later, and one of them, reports Hinde, shows signs of permanent emotional disturbance. Where human babies are concerned, one feels that a one in four risk would still be indefensible.

Some American studies of maternal deprivation in young monkeys, by Harlow, are also of much interest. These were raised under a variety of conditions, with different allowances of mothering, play with age mates and the like. Some were raised by artificial mothers, which differed in maternal attributes such as warmth, a nipple providing milk, and a soft covering to which the baby monkeys liked to cling. The latter was found to be of great importance: the babies spent more time clinging to this mother-substitute than to the food-providing, but not cuddly, one.

Young monkeys raised by the 'cuddly' mother substitute appeared to develop normally, both physically and emotionally. But none of the males, when adult, was able to mate successfully. A few of the females were, however, fertilised (by normal males), and these proved totally inadequate as mothers. When the baby struggled desperately to cling to the mother, the latter brushed it off like a fly, and sometimes even trod on it.

The question again arises: what inferences can we validly make, from experiments of this kind, to human beings? In my view, at least part of the answer is clear. If certain conditions have been shown to be harmful for other animals, and particularly for primates—our closest relatives—then to be sure we cannot be *certain* that they will also be harmful for human young. But in the absence of evidence to the contrary, the only safe assumption is that they are: and if anyone wishes to argue that these conditions are harmless to human children (say, because of their greater adaptability), then the burden of proof must rest on them.

One other group of animal studies is of interest in relation to possible parallels in human development. These are of *imprinting*, which was referred to briefly in the first section: and they are described by Lorenz in his very readable book, *King Solomon's Ring*. We have space here for only two examples.

The auditory response of young Greylag goslings to the quacking of their mother is innate, and they will follow this sound whoever or whatever is making it. The visual attachment to their mother is, however, learnt shortly after hatching. There is a critical period, the first few hours after hatching, when they will attach themselves to the experimenter if he handles them, or quacks like a duck; and thereafter they will follow him about, squat under his chair, and totally ignore their real mother. The effect is irreversible, and the birds when adult will not mate with their kind. They may, however, try to mate with the experimenter, as was the case with a jackdaw hand-raised by Lorenz.

This imprinting would therefore appear to be, at least in some animals, a crucial factor of social learning, which decides for life whether the individual will seek the company of its own species or not. The possible implications for humans are naturally of great interest. It has been suggested, for example, that human babies form an attachment to their mother by imprinting at some early age, and that the irreversibility of this is a factor of the well-known difficulty of successful adoption. It certainly seems possible that imprinting takes place in humans, but on this we have at present no clear evidence.

Play

From an adult point of view, children's play may seem undirected, and aimless in terms of the real world. The word 'play', for most of us, means something we do just for pleasure: as opposed to work, which we do because we need to, or in pursuit of a long-term goal.

To see it in this way is entirely to miss its real significance. Play is one of the chief ways by which children learn. It is self-directed learning, which is why adults do not always see the point of it. But this means that it is learning for its own sake, which (as was said at the end of the last section but one) is one of the most important forms of human learning.

Children develop their motor abilities by play. They are continually seeking out new things to do—walls to walk along and jump off, tables to climb on and crawl under, chairs to tip over and use as ladders, ladders to lay flat and balance on the rungs. Their movements lack the economy of adults—jumping off a climbing frame, they may continue into a forward roll, waving their legs joyfully in the air to finish. This is movement for its own sake, so far as the children are concerned, not for the gaining of some particular end. But all the time they are gaining in control, balance, co-ordination, as well as developing their muscles and lungs, and increasing their metabolic rate.

One of the most important things in man's history has been the use of tools: and children learn the use of tools by play. A stick is one of the most primitive, but also one of the most versatile, of tools, which we still use in many forms to extend our reach (e.g. a gear lever of a car), keep our hands out of harm's way (e.g. poke the fire) and as the basis of the lever. A child with a stick is finding this out by stirring puddles and bringing up leaves from the bottom, poking under and through other objects, rattling it along the railings.

Play is a major area of social learning. By playing with their contemporaries, children gradually learn to co-operate, take turns, see other people's point of view. Many factors are at work here. A shared interest has a great cohesive effect, so children playing together in a sandpit, or playing with model cars, are already under an influence which makes for harmony. The wise parent tries to reduce disruptive influences by making sure that there is plenty of play material for everybody. The younger children play together, but independently. Soon, however, they want to make a 'tent', or carry something too heavy for one alone, and co-operation is required. This develops most easily out of a shared goal, but gradually (and not without occasional friction) children learn to co-operate even when there is some conflict of interests—for example, to take turns on a swing. 'Fair turns' is an important stage in socialisation, since it involves the postponement of gratification, and the subordination of an immediate wish to a long-term one—that of being accepted by playfellows.

After the informal games of early childhood, the next stage is that of games with rules, such as conkers, hopscotch, tig, hide and seek, leading on to the highly structured games continued into adult life such as cricket and football. (The latter are of greater value developmentally when they are still child-governed: 'compulsory games', controlled by adults, appear to me as a contradiction in terms.) In a now classical study of the game of marbles as played by children in Geneva and Neuchatel, Piaget found, as children grew older, a developing awareness of the value of rules for co-operation to the benefit of all. As one boy well expressed it, 'So as not to be always quarrelling one must have rules, and then play properly.' Piaget also found that the younger children, who regarded rules as absolute, unalterable, almost of divine origin, cheated much more freely than the older ones who recognised that they had grown up by mutual agreement, and could be changed in the same way. There seems to be a moral here for families, schools and indeed all social institutions!

The imaginative play of children is another activity of much greater developmental importance than most adults realise. It has two chief aspects—symbolic and role-playing. In symbolic play, children find that 'things can stand for other things': a box for a garage, or blanket over two chairs for a house, a stick for a gun. In this, they are repeating one of the most important discoveries of mankind— symbolic representation. To begin with, the symbols are concrete objects having some resemblance to those which they represent. But there is also a verbal link—the stick is *called* a gun—and this emphasises the conceptual aspect. It is by being *thought of* as a gun, even more than by looking like a gun, that a stick can satisfyingly be used as one in a game of cowboys and Indians. Surprisingly early, the concrete props can be discarded on occasion. I recently played an elaborate make-believe with a child aged three and a half, involving the cooking of an egg by each of us, cutting the top off, and eating it, entirely by mime and words. Play of this kind is a stepping-stone to the development of new actions by mental experiment, and thus indirectly to some of the greatest technical achievements of man.

During imaginative play, children also take on the roles of other people—mothers and fathers, shopkeepers, bus drivers, doctors and nurses. This helps to develop the ability to see things from the point of view of others, which is important for both social and cognitive development. Children sometimes also use role-playing to help themselves to assimilate frightening experiences. A little girl aged about seven, just back from hospital, spent much time playing at being a nurse for two or three weeks afterwards: taking temperatures, making beds, washing, and also freely admonishing her imaginary patients to be good and get better quickly. She was reliving a time in which she had been passive and relatively helpless, but with the situation reversed. This made her feel better about it.

Resembling this is cathartic play—the use of play as an

excuse, or disguise, by which to express feelings which otherwise might be unacceptable either to other people or to the child himself. Aggression can be worked off harmlessly by playing at cops and robbers; resentment towards authority, and also the desire to wield the power of authority, in games of 'school'. Here we are near the realm of play therapy, a form of psychotherapy in which children are encouraged to play freely with a variety of suitable material, ranging from sand and water to dolls representing mother, father and children, in a doll's house complete with bathroom and lavatory. Such play is both diagnostic and therapeutic, and is widely used in child psychotherapy. But its value is not confined to 'problem children': suitable play material and facilities are also useful prophylactics.

In its many varieties, play can thus be seen to be one of the most important ways in which children learn. We may well ask ourselves at what age, if any, does play cease to be important? Must we not all learn, at some stage, to work— to apply ourselves to the necessary though unattractive task? And if so, surely the sooner we start to learn this, the better?

Part of the answer to these questions is that psychology, like other sciences, is not concerned with the questions involving 'must', 'ought', 'better', but with observing, explaining, predicting. Observation of child behaviour leads to the conclusion that play is one of the most effective ways in which children do learn. What use is made of this information is the particular province of parents and teachers, whose decisions are based on value judgements held by them as individuals and as members of society. It is significant, however, that play-like methods are being used more and more in primary schools. At the other extreme, though university research can hardly be described as play, nevertheless it does seem to share something of the same quality, in that it is a free exploration of the environment pursued largely for its own sake. Perhaps we could all learn more efficiently, as well as more enjoyably, if we knew how to use deliberately the same kinds of approach as children use intuitively in their play.

RICHARD R. SKEMP

The Concept of Intelligence

Like other sciences, psychology takes words from everyday speech, and gives them a specialised meaning. Usually the meaning given is more restricted and more precise. Unfortunately, this is not so for intelligence, of which there seem to be nearly as many definitions as there are psychologists who write about this topic. Binet, originator of what is still one of the most widely used intelligence tests, wrote that it was fundamentally 'judgement, otherwise called good sense, practical sense, initiative, the faculty of adapting oneself to circumstances. To judge well, to comprehend well, to reason well, these are the essential activities of intelligence.' Spearman, pioneer of the statistical approach, regarded his factor *g* as 'the eduction of relations and correlates'. Piaget, widely known for his work in developmental psychology, describes it as 'an equilibrium between assimilation and accommodation'. It would be easy to fill a page with other definitions, all by leading psychologists, all different. Knight offers: 'the capacity of relational, constructive thinking, directed to the attainment of some end'. Vernon decides that 'probably ... the best definition we can give is a rather simple non-specific one', such as 'all-round thinking capacities', or 'mental efficiency'. Hebb makes a valuable distinction between 'Intelligence A', the innate potential, and 'Intelligence B', the actual mental ability at a given time. All we can observe and try to measure is 'Intelligence B'; but there is good evidence in support of Intelligence A as one important factor of Intelligence B, others being its interaction with the environment from birth onwards, and the present physical and emotional state of the subject. Yet another definition is that of Terman, co-author of the most widely used revision of Binet's original intelligence test. He said that intelligence was the individual's capacity to think abstractedly and use abstract symbols: a definition which applies well enough to advanced academic activity, but seems to exclude the kind of shrewd judgement in everyday affairs which most people would also regard as indicative of intelligence.

Finally, we may look at some of the many available intelligence tests, and try to decide from the items just what it is that they are testing. Here are a few examples:

From Terman-Merrill: *'In what ways are a cricket ball and an orange alike, and in what ways are they different?'*

From Wechsler's intelligence scale for children: *'What should you do if you see a train approaching a broken track?'*

A typical item from a test used for selection at eleven plus: *Underline the word which does not belong with the others: wall, fence, hedge, road, railing.*

Two important questions seem to be: can we find anything in common among all the foregoing? And can we explain why intelligence is a good thing to have? The second question is not as naïve as it sounds. In spite of the extensive use of intelligence tests to select those who are most capable of profiting from higher education, no one (to my knowledge) has clearly stated why intelligence as measured by intelligence tests enables people to learn better. Indeed, Vernon goes so far as to say: 'It is obvious, for example, that our current intelligence tests make no attempt to measure modifiability or learning capacity as such.' So to ask what is the connexion between intelligence and learning is no idle question.

It is the present writer's view that first, the everyday notion of intelligence as the ability to act appropriately in a variety of different circumstances is basically sound; second, that the connexions between this and intelligence as tested, and between the latter and ability to learn, are fundamentally straightforward.

One of the requirements for appropriate activity, in any given set of circumstances, is to be able to take into account all relevant factors, and to relate them to each other and to the desired goal. The essential factor here is the ability to relate.

Another requirement is the bringing of past experience to bear on present problems. To do this efficiently requires that this experience be classified, so that each new event can be seen as like a certain class of earlier experiences in some ways, unlike in others. These classes may be quite distinct; or they may overlap, or fall one within another, or form hierarchies. For example, a bus and a lorry are alike in being motor vehicles, and unlike in that one will halt at a bus stop and not the other. Both classes belong to many larger classes, such as those of motor vehicles, means of transport, and potentially lethal instruments. We can behave appropriately because we can classify correctly. Classification is one particular kind of relating: and forming relationships between classes, another.

Appropriate behaviour thus involves relating each new event to an organised mental structure derived from past experiences. The ability to build up such a structure is equivalent to the ability to relate experiences one to another, class to class: and the better organised the structure, the more swiftly and efficiently can relevant experience be brought to bear, and the greater is the variety of experience from which a useful contribution can be derived.

Such an organisation of knowledge has been called a *schema* by Bartlett, Piaget and others.

It has two major functions: to relate and organise existing knowledge, and to act as a mental tool for the acquisition of new knowledge. Learning never starts from nothing: it is always dependent on the existence of some other ability, innate or learnt. This is so from the highest to the most primitive forms of learning. Learning the principles of aircraft design depends on a prior knowledge of (among other things) fluid dynamics, which requires advanced knowledge of calculus, which depends on algebra, which depends on arithmetic. The last itself is acquired, like so much else, by the use of speech. And the ability of a suckling baby to reach for and seize his bottle, put the teat in his mouth and suck it, depends on pre-existing schemata such as visual fixation, reaching, grasping. Since two different modalities are involved, relating these is quite an achievement: as anyone who has watched a growing baby can see.

In schematic learning, new information is not just added

to, but assimilated to and becomes part of, the existing structure of knowledge. This cannot be over-emphasised, since it is the chief feature of intelligent learning. *We can learn by relating new experiences to what we know already.*

This ability to relate is, in the present writer's view, the essence of intelligence, and it seems to cover all, or nearly all, the aspects of intelligence emphasised by the definitions quoted earlier. 'Intelligence B', as revealed by appropriate behaviour in a given situation (which may be a complex problem situation) will depend on the existence of appropriate schemas. A highly intelligent electronics engineer, and an equally intelligent economist, might fail hopelessly at problems in each other's fields of knowledge. 'Intelligence B' is related to a particular context.

So what do we mean by supposing that these two are equally intelligent? We might mean that they were capable of solving equally difficult problems in their respective fields—but how can we equate the difficulty of such different tasks? An alternative meaning would be that they both had high 'Intelligence A', as revealed by their ability to build up their respective schemas: an activity continuous, in both of them, since birth. Moreover, this ability to build up complex schemas, dependent in turn on the ability to relate, may reasonably be supposed to be ultimately dependent on innate neural organisations: so the hereditary aspect of intelligence can be fitted in with this approach.

There is space here to discuss only two more aspects of intelligence, emphasised respectively by the definitions of Terman and of Piaget. Terman's considered that intelligence was the individual's capacity to think abstractly, and use abstract symbols. What do we mean by an abstraction? It is something common to a class of experiences, or it is a relationship between classes, or it may represent a class of classes. *Using* these abstractions makes possible the 'judgement, good sense, practical sense', included in Binet's definition. But an abstract symbol stands for the common property, or relationship, itself. These are objects of thought, not external objects. So the ability to think abstractly involves the ability of the mind to turn inward on itself, to reflect on its own ideas. This reflective intelligence may perhaps be considered as a particular class of 'Intelligence B'—a large class, including among others all the sciences. The so-called 'absent minded professor' may be concentrating on the activity of reflective intelligence. I do not know—I have not met one.

The view of intelligence here put forward is closely related to the biological idea of intelligence as manifested in adaptability. We have stressed the assimilation of new knowledge to existing schemata: but must now turn our attention to a complementary activity of the schema, whereby it must itself become modified in the process. This is called *accommodation*, and as Piaget has pointed out assimilation and accommodaion are two aspects of the same process. The first emphasises the integration of new knowledge with existing schemata; the second, the development of the schema which results. Accommodation may also take the form of a restructuring of the existing schema, necessary before assimilation can take place. For example, Piaget quotes the instance of a child who thought that the moon followed him overhead as he walked. He was asked whether it did the same for a friend, walking in a different direction. This new problem could not successfully be dealt with by the child's existing schema—it had to undergo a basic change.

This more difficult kind of accommodation requires the ability not only to form relationships but to change them where necessary for new ones. Is some other aspect of intelligence now involved, describable as flexibility, open-mindedness? We do not yet know: but there are certainly times when obstinacy, prejudice or fear, cause intelligent people to behave unintelligently. It is also well known that children will score below their true ability at an intelligence test if they are anxious, or ill at ease with the person who is testing them. These interactions between emotional factors and intelligence are still too little understood, and are an important area for future research.

Rationale of Mental Testing

An aim of any science is to use measurement as a basis for comparison, prediction and control. This has been achieved with very great accuracy in most of the natural sciences. We can weigh a pencil dot on a piece of paper, measure the thickness of a spider's thread or the ten-thousandth part of a second. This has had several unfortunate repercussions on psychology. One is an assumption by non-psychologists that, say, an intelligence quotient of 116 can be regarded as accurate to the nearest whole number: whereas it really means 'somewhere between about 113 and 119, at the time when this subject was tested'.

Another mistaken assumption, common this time among psychologists, is that observations cannot be regarded as scientific unless they can in some way be subjected to mathematical (preferably statistical) analysis. But in all sciences, taxonomy (classification) must precede measurement. To measure is to compare observations of a particular quality with unit quantities of the same quality—we do not try to measure weight in units of temperature. So these qualities must first be isolated, and their interactions determined. If we try to measure how much oxygen there is in a closed litre jar by determining its volume, we could easily arrive at the same measure for 1·4 gm or 0·14 gm of the gas by weight, unless we knew the interactions of volume, temperature and pressure. Even when these results were known, physicists were still led astray by the presence of isotopes having different atomic weights. The difficulty of isolating the qualities to be measured, and finding how they interact, is enormously greater for the psychologist: not least because what is observed is liable to be altered by the mere fact of being under observation. Some of the most important pioneering work has, therefore, been in the analysis of the processes involved, and the ways in which the contributory factors interact. The work of two of the greatest psychologists of this century, Freud and Piaget, has been entirely qualitative, not quantitative.

Both in everyday life and in the other sciences, measurement involves the use of units. Numbers come originally from counting how many separate objects there are in a given collection: and measurement consists of turning the question 'How much?' into the question, 'How many units?' We are then making use of the cardinal property of number.

When measuring psychological qualities, however, units are impossible to define. What is a unit of intelligence, or of extraversion? All we can do, when we think we have isolated a quality and found some behaviour directly dependent on this quality, is to arrange people's performances in order of magnitude: number of items correctly answered in an intelligence scale, number of questions answered in a direction indicative of extraversion. We are then making use of the *ordinal* property of number. This enables us to compare people with each other, in relation to this quality: but the numbers we have cannot validly be added, subtracted or multiplied in the same way as cardinal numbers. An I.Q. of 100 means that a person's score at the intelligence test is equivalent to the average for his age. But we cannot meaningfully add two I.Q.s of 100 in the same way as we can add two weights or lengths. We can meaningfully say that someone with an I.Q. of 100 is more intelligent than someone with an I.Q. of 90, but not that he is twice as intelligent as someone with an I.Q. of 50.

Two assumptions which are taken for granted in everyday measurement are that our measuring instruments are reliable, and valid. That is to say, we assume that our rulers, kitchen scales and clocks do not vary from day to day, nor according to the user; and that they do in fact measure length, weight and time. These requirements have not been achieved without a certain amount of research; and in psychology, this research is still in progress.

We might check the reliability of a psychological test by repeating it on the same subject, to see if he gets the same score. The objection to this is that he might very likely find the test easier when doing it for the second time. To get over this difficulty parallel forms of the same test are sometimes developed, and these are very useful for retesting someone after a period to see whether there has been any change.

The construction of a psychological test is, however, a lengthy business, and we do not always want to double the work. The difficulty can be neatly overcome by finding what is called the split half reliability of the test. The scores on the odd items are correlated with those on the even items, for a large number of subjects. This gives a measure of the internal consistency of the test which is widely used.

We still do not know whether our intelligence test really measures intelligence. It could be entirely reliable, in the above sense: and still measure something different from intelligence. The difficulty of confirming the validity of a test is even greater when we are trying to measure other qualities such as extraversion/introversion, cyclothymia (emotionally expressive, frank, placid)/schizothymia (reserved, close-mouthed, anxious), to quote just two examples from many. In general, we try to observe whether people behave in the ways which we would predict from these scores. This is easier in some cases than in others. From people who score highly in intelligence tests, we would, for example, predict better examination results. This is, broadly, confirmed: but the results are not clear-cut because of other factors which also affect examination performance, such as home background (whether parents encourage children to work), and emotional factors. Yet intelligence tests are among the easiest kind to validate, far easier than personality tests.

The emphasis of this section has been largely on the difficulties of mental testing, in order that these may not be underestimated. But by much painstaking research, based on an appreciation of the problems involved, steady progress is being made in overcoming them.

Behavioural Disorders

The first thing to get clear is that behaviour disorders are not necessarily the same as behaviours which are troublesome to adults. The normal young child is noisy, dirty, inquisitive, untidy and self-willed. One who is quiet, clean, doesn't touch things that aren't his, incurious, tidy and obedient, may be 'no trouble at all': but is more likely to need psychological help later on than the former.

Nevertheless, educational pressures from parents and teachers are, necessarily, steadily directed towards teaching children to control the first kind of behaviour—in brief, towards socialising them. A large group of behavioural disorders can be ascribed to this socialising process being either unsuccessful, or over-successful. In the first case we say that the child is delinquent, or anti-social; in the second we say that he is neurotic. (The other main group of behavioural disorders, resulting from organic disease or subnormality, will be discussed under the heading of 'The Handicapped Child'.)

The degree of socialisation which we expect depends, of course, on age. If a two-year-old helps himself to a toy which takes his fancy, without regard to whose property it is, we regard this as normal. We would hardly call it stealing in a five-year-old, though by now we are trying to teach him the difference between mine and thine. In a twelve-year-old, we would regard persistent theft as a behaviour problem. He has taken too long to learn this social norm.

On the other hand, they may be learnt too completely. Games like football are a useful outlet for aggression, and socially accepted to the extent of being almost a requirement. A boy whose aggression has been suppressed too completely will not have enough available even to play football successfully, so in this case socialisation has, by being over-successful, partially defeated its own ends.

We see that socialisation is partly a matter of timing, partly also of directing an instinct into useful channels rather than suppressing it.

Behaviour problems may result from under-learning or over-learning; and there is a third category, those due to wrong learning. Some children learn either delinquent or neurotic traits from their parents, and the social group in which they grow up. Petty theft, destructiveness, inter-gang aggressiveness, are all normal features of certain 'delinquent sub-cultures', and children will acquire them in the course of adaptation to environments of this kind. Parents, contemporaries, or both, may serve as models for delinquent behaviour. Highly respectable parents, too, may unconsciously 'cue' children into misbehaviour. While apparently reproving them, e.g. for lack of submission to authority while at school, they may do so in such a way that their child, 'reading between the lines', can perceive that they really rather admire this behaviour. Or by telling others in front of the child that he has (e.g.) eating problems, they may create difficulties where none previously existed. Parental response to normal sexual curiosity and exploration may, instead of providing matter-of-fact information (including where appropriate the information that some behaviours are not generally approved) cause children to feel uniquely depraved.

It is currently fashionable to blame parents for all that goes wrong in a child's development, while absolving the child from responsibility. Certainly their influence is crucial: but innate characteristics of the children must also be taken into account. Further, parents' attitudes to their children are greatly influenced by their earlier relationships with their own parents: so who was responsible for these? Psychologically, it is more useful to stop worrying about responsibility, and look for causes. When these are identified, suitable remedies may then be found.

For children, the latter fall into three broad categories: training, play therapy and environmental therapy. Training means providing the suitable learning conditions whereby the missed learning can be made up—e.g. remedial reading: non-readers are likely to show behaviour problems in later childhood. Play therapy, already mentioned, can be diagnostic, cathartic, and also enable a child through repetition to come to terms with situations (e.g. a stay in hospital) and feelings (e.g. destructiveness) which were previously experienced as threats. Environmental therapy is based on trying to trace the environmental factors which are causing the trouble, and advising parents about changing these.

It may be comforting to note, in conclusion, that some degree of 'naughtiness' is to be regarded as a normal part of development. When a group of students at a college of education were questioned in confidence about their past, almost all were found to have indulged at some time in behaviour which, if detected, would have been treated as 'delinquent'. All were now on the way to becoming pillars of society. Some deviations from the normal need give no cause for alarm: others, however, should be taken seriously. Johnson and Medinnus list as behaviour problems with a high probability of remission, among others: timidity, tantrums, eneuresis, social delinquency, excessive demanding of attention; and among those with a low probability of remission they include nail-biting, depression, solitary delinquency, unresponsiveness, excessive modesty.

The Handicapped Child

Perhaps the greatest problem of handicapped children is that they will grow into handicapped adults. The normal impulse to care for and protect any child is intensified, in most, by the sight of a child who is physically or mentally handicapped. Fewer show this response to a handicapped adult. While he is a child, special care will be forthcoming from parents, institutions and teachers; but as an adult, in most cases he will have to look after himself, and if possible to earn his own living. Even the pity which is shown him can be harmful if it is the wrong kind: for, as the novelist Stefan Zweig has pointed out, it may be little more than a desire to rid oneself of the discomfort caused by the sight of another's misfortune. Underlying this kind of pity is an unconscious rejection which is liable to emphasise the handicapped child's feeling that he is not like other children. We all need to feel accepted by our fellows as one of them, and this need is greater, not less, for the handicapped.

Few people are able to behave quite normally towards a child (or other person) who is in some way abnormal. And by this I do not mean ignoring the handicap, but behaving realistically towards it—accepting it for what it is, no more, and no less. These side-effects, which is to say the social and psychological problems, may well be harder to overcome than the handicap itself. This is partly because they are problems of society itself, which has less motivation to grapple with them than the affected individual.

Overt rejection is now much rarer than it was. Over-compensation is probably a greater danger, particularly for the parents, whose normal urge to cherish and protect their child is intensified both naturally by its greater need, and possibly also by a defensive process of reaction-formation to overcome and conceal even from themselves their wish that they had not been afflicted with such a child. The former component is appropriate and useful, since his requirements in care, time and patience will be even greater than for a normal child. The latter, though equally understandable, is a result of the needs of the parents, not of the child, and it may result in over-protection, too much help, thereby making it even harder for the child to achieve the maximum independence of which he is capable. It is difficult to stand by and let a blind child suffer the bumps inevitable while learning to find his way about, or to let a crippled child drag himself painfully upstairs instead of carrying him. This needs not only patience and sympathy but a slightly tough-minded attitude: the first two being towards the child, and the last towards his handicap. Normal growing-up contains many problems. The handicapped child has more problems, and lessened resources for dealing with them. So he will need more help and encouragement; but he will also have to try harder, and make more use of what he has. And in adult life, this state of affairs will be intensified.

So far, no distinction has been made between the different kinds of handicap. To deal separately with these would need several books, and it has therefore been thought more appropriate here to concentrate on some of the general psychological problems. But it is interesting to note, as Kershaw points out in his excellent book *Handicapped Children*, how widely different are the general attitudes to people with different handicaps. Blindness evokes nothing but sympathy, whereas deafness is often regarded with a mixture of amusement and contempt. This may be partly because we all have some idea what it is like to be blind, from having tried to find our way in the dark, or merely by closing our eyes. We do not commonly experience loss of hearing in the same kind of way. Probably another major factor is the impairment of communication, which is far greater in the deaf than in the blind. There may also be reasons why mental handicap has been among the last to be accepted with understanding. We feel that we could still be ourselves with the same mind in an impaired body, but not vice versa; so it is much harder to regard the mentally abnormal as one of ourselves.

Behind this there may be an intuitive awareness of a deeper truth, that it is only by communication and interaction with other humans that we become fully human. (This is shown by studies of feral children—human children separated from their kind soon after birth, and raised by animals, and who remain in their mental processes and behaviour essentially subhuman.) But this only means that where there is impairment of communication due to any kind of handicap, sensory or mental, there is an even greater need for the best quality and quantity of communication through whatever channels remain; and a greater onus on the rest of us to provide it.

Summary

Man may well be described as a new breakthrough in evolution, due to our enormously greater ability to learn: the difference being qualitative as well as quantitative. This gives us adaptability beyond that of any other species, and an increasing power to change the physical environment to suit ourselves. The price we pay for these abilities is a much longer period of dependence; and the more advanced the culture, the longer it usually is.

During this period, we learn the knowledge and skills necessary to live in the particular physical and social environment into which we are born. Some of this learning is intentional on our part; some is intended by those who educate us (parents, teachers and others); some—perhaps the greater part—is neither. In the last category, play is a way of learning whose importance is only slowly being realised.

The relative contributions of heredity and environment to the character and abilities of an adult are the subject of continuing argument and experiment. Perhaps a more fruitful approach would be to study the nature of their interaction. Intelligence, for example, may usefully be regarded as the ability to interact with the environment in particularly adaptive ways, by classifying one's experiences, relating these categories to each other, storing and communicating them with the help of symbols.

Successfully adjusting to our fellow humans is another major task of childhood, and a major factor of our happiness. Here, too, parents play a decisive role. They teach us how we may and may not acceptably satisfy our basic drives; and from them, we first learn to love and be loved.

The importance of developmental psychology is not restricted to those concerned with the upbringing of children —though sooner or later this happens to most of us. Our present selves are built on our earlier selves, and at no stage can we detach ourselves from the influences of our formative years. So in learning better to understand children, we are also learning more about ourselves.

Suggested Reading

BOWLBY, J., *Child Care and the Growth of Love*, London: Penguin, 1953.

BOWLEY, A. H., *The Young Handicapped Child*, Edinburgh and London: Livingstone, 1957.

FREUD, ANNA, *Introduction to Psycho-Analysis for Teachers*, London: Allen & Unwin, 1931.

HALDANE, J. B. S., and HUXLEY, J., *Animal Biology, chapters* IX–XIII (for evolutionary background), Oxford: Clarendon, 1927.

MUSSEN, P. H., *The Psychological Development of the Child*, (Foundation of Modern Psychology series: paperback), New Jersey: Prentice-Hall, 1963.

PIAGET, J., *The Moral Judgement of the Child*, London: Kegan Paul, 1932.

VERNON, P. E., *Intelligence and Attainment Tests*, University of London Press, 1960.

5

Language And Communication

R. C. Oldfield

Introduction

Rather suddenly, the study of language and communication has become widespread and has taken on a new tempo. Linguists, physiologists, engineers and psychologists have all become involved, sometimes independently, sometimes in friendly if turbulent collaboration. The main reason is that, in an increasingly complex and interconnected world, the need for communication of all kinds has rapidly grown. But as better means are devised these facilities themselves further increase the complexity and stimulate renewed demands.

Only a hundred years or so ago most people rarely spoke to any but their immediate neighbours and were often unable to read or write. Now an increasing number of people have to communicate with others by telephone, letter or printed page, and sometimes in a foreign tongue. One result has been a profound change, and increasing standardisation, in language itself. Another is that the individual who is subject to any handicap or disablement in his use of language, whether this lies in himself or in his immediate circumstances, is at an increasingly grave disadvantage. A word-blind child, a partially deaf adult, a man whose speech has been damaged by injury or disease of the brain, are all sadly affected. Again, people more frequently have to communicate in the presence of noise, or while bombarded with a multiplicity of messages, only one of which they must attend to and act on. More and more of the world's workers have to

I   117

communicate with machines such as computers, in strange artificial languages. Even that prevalent and well-accoutred contemporary, the Business Executive, now finds knowledge of a foreign tongue vital in the Export Drive.

But in all these many connexions we still know hardly anything of the psychological and physiological processes involved. Help for people who in one way or another are linguistically disabled too often depends on what is optimistically described as an 'empirical' basis—all too often a cover for hide-bound conviction. Language laboratories spring up everywhere to teach people foreign languages, but practically nothing is known of what goes on psychologically when they learn them. Computer science and practice threaten to outstrip our powers of communicating with their hardware products. We do know a little of the factors which affect communication in noisy or otherwise difficult conditions, but we still have only the most rudimentary theories about how the brain manages this or, indeed, anything else to do with speech and writing.

So, even leaving aside the intrinsic fascination of the problems, there is plenty of practical impetus for both research and its application. There are opportunities for people of many different kinds and varied backgrounds which offer scope for individual or collaborative work in the laboratory, the library and the hospital. The last section of this chapter gives some idea of these opportunities, and of the roads by which they may be gained.

So far as research is concerned, too much is going on for adequate summary. Perhaps the best thing is for me to describe what a few representative workers might be doing and why.

Making Do With Less Speech

Consider the question of *how much* of the speech-wave we need to hear in order to understand what is said. When we listen to a speaker he is often interrupted by noises, or he may speak too softly for us to catch every word. There is an ulterior practical motive for research into these questions because telephone lines and radio links are scarce and expensive. If we needed only to send a small fraction of the speech wave at regular intervals it might be possible to stick similar fractions of other conversations in between whiles. (This in fact turns out to be possible, and something like a hundred simultaneous conversations can now be sent down the same line by this means.) To avoid getting in tangles straight away with the *redundancies* in speech due to grammar, syntax and a continuous context which make guessing possible, standardised lists of single words are used. The *intelligibility* is measured by the percentage of

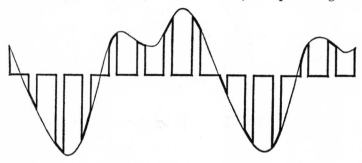

Fig. 1 Effect of periodic interruption (on–off 1:2) on acoustic wave. Original wave in light, resultant in heavy, outline

words correctly heard and written down. The subject of the experiment hears these words through telephones and it is arranged that, by means of an electronic box, the speech current to them is cut off regularly at a certain rate which can be controlled, and for a certain fraction of the time, in the fashion shown in Figure 1. The rate of interruption is varied from once every five seconds to ten thousand times a second and the proportion of time during which the speech reaches the ears of the hearer from $6\frac{1}{4}$ to 75 per cent.

The graph in Figure 2 shows the results of this experiment. It may seem surprising that we can still get over 60 per cent intelligibility if we take away three-quarters of the speech sound twenty times a second. Whether or not a word is correctly heard depends on whether what is left of it allows us to discriminate it from other words. But it is at least clear that speech sounds are far richer than we need them to be. It may seem even more surprising that we can actually remove over 90 per cent of the speech-wave and still get very nearly 100 per cent intelligibility, provided we do this at a very high interruption rate of some ten thousand a second.

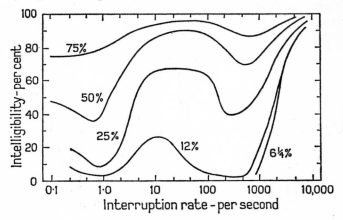

Fig. 2 Effect of speech interruption on intelligibility. Separate curves show various percentages of time on. Based on J. C. R. Licklider and G. A. Miller, 'The Perception of Speech', in S. S. Stevens (ed.), *Handbook of Experimental Psychology*, New York: Wiley, 1951

In fact, this is quite in keeping with what is known from other experiments on the contributions of different frequency components in the speech to its intelligibility. The higher frequencies are of the greater importance (though they contribute very little to the loudness) and it is these frequencies which are preserved in this particular kind of interruption.

This sort of experiment exemplifies one kind of method which may be used in exploring the processes of speech perception. But our experimenter might equally well have been interested in degrading the speech in another way. He might decide to add a lot of noise to it and see how the proportion of noise to signal affected the intelligibility. If he does this, using a standard intelligibility test, he gets a curve like c in Figure 3. But he can now make a start with estimating the effects which *connexions* between words have.

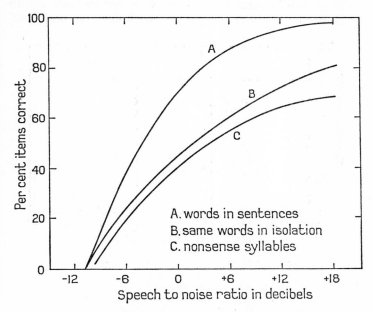

Fig. 3 Effect of contextual connection on intelligibility. (Based on G. A. Miller, G. A. Heise and W. Lichter, 'The intelligibility of speech as a function of the context of the test material', *Journal of Experimental Psychology*, 1951. XLI, 329–35.

For instance, if the sequence of words forms a meaningful passage, then it is far more impervious to noise and he will get a curve like A, while if he jumbles up all these same words, the effect will be much closer to that shown for the independent words of the intelligibility test B. The meaningful sequence, which has grammatical structure and context, is easier to hear because a good deal can be 'guessed' even though it is missing. Even the same words jumbled up are better off than the independent ones because of their contextual association, and because they occur in the right kind of proportions.

The experimenter may go a little farther and try to estimate the effect of contextual association. He now com-

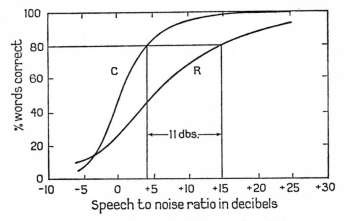

Fig. 4 Effect of common reference of words in
intelligibility test.
R—Randomly chosen words
C—Words standing for parts of the body
(Based on D. J. Bruce, 'Speech Engineering', in
Science News, 44, Penguin Books, 1957)

pares intelligibility for a given set of *randomly chosen* words with that for the same number of words which have some sort of *common reference*. For instance, the latter set of words might all have to do with food or travelling or politics. Once again, these contextually related words have an advantage over the random, which can be seen in Figure 4. It is interesting that this advantage begins to be shown before the subject has consciously grasped the relationship between the words. But the important point about this kind of experiment is that it gives us a method of assessing *quantitatively* the effect of factors which we wish to know about. We may take, say, the 80 per cent level of intelligibility and read off the difference of noise levels. Thus, in this latter experiment, it seems as if the effect of common reference is the equivalent of 11 decibels of noise. This is a simple illustration of how we can introduce quantification into the comparison of linguistic factors which are themselves not directly measurable.

The Cocktail Party Problem

Another experimenter is at work on a rather more complex topic. She is trying to find out how, when our ears are assailed with a multitude of voices and messages, our brains can sort them out and allow us to pay attention, and respond, to only one of them. This is really more of a puzzle than it might seem at first sight, because the result of all the talk around us is a *single* very complex sound wave which goes into our ears. How does the brain filter one message out from this and reject the rest?

This problem was first looked into about fifteen years ago using a simple and straightforward technique. The subject wears headphones, a message is put into one ear and a second message into the other. To get positive data the subject is instructed to repeat aloud continuously what he hears in one specified ear. His version is taken down on a tape-recorder, and his score is the number of errors he makes. With only a single message everyone can carry out this task —'shadowing' it is called—after only a very small amount of practice. When a second message competes for the subject's attention his performance is less good, and the effects of different factors can be compared in terms of the corresponding error-scores. It is, for instance, much easier to shadow a male voice if the competing message is spoken by a female than when both voices are male, particularly if they are the same voice. Similarly a difference of loudness between the two signals is helpful in itself though, as might be expected, it is much better if the message to be shadowed is the louder, than when the one to be rejected is, though within limits even this can be more favourable than equality. By putting both messages into both ears in differing reciprocal proportions we can make them seem to come from *different directions* and, as one might expect once again, the ease of shadowing is greatly affected by the separation of the apparent directions from which they come. Another interesting result from simple experiments such as these is that the message to be rejected seems to be filtered out with astonishing completeness. Provided the voice remains the same, the subject is quite unaware if the language of the rejected message is suddenly changed to another, foreign, one. Nor does he become aware that the two messages are, in fact, the same if their timing differs by more than a quarter of a second with the rejected message leading, and about a second and a half if it lags. (These figures tell us something about the time during which the messages are retained in the immediate memory store while they are being processed.)

Such experiments, however, are confined to variation of the purely acoustic features of the signals. What happens if these acoustic features are made as far as possible identical? The filtering process then becomes very much more difficult: nevertheless, it is still possible.

This means that there must be another filtering system which operates not on *acoustic* but on *linguistic* cues. Such things as continuity of theme and context, the constraints imposed by rules of grammar and syntax, and in general the differing probabilities of one word rather than another following any given sequence all play a part. It is to these questions that our research worker is addressing herself, and she adopts two different approaches. The first is to ring the changes on the message which is to be *rejected*. This can be chosen so as to be to a greater or less extent familiar to the subject as regards its language or its content. So she does an experiment in which the message to be shadowed is always a narrative or descriptive extract from a novel read by a woman, while the message to be rejected is one of the following:

1. A passage from the same novel in a man's voice.

2. A passage from the same novel in the same woman's voice as the shadowed message is spoken in.

3. A passage from a technical discussion of biochemistry in the woman's voice.

4. A passage from a French novel in the woman's voice.

5. A passage in the Czech language spoken with a deliberately English accent (equivalent to nonsense using the same phonemes as English) in the woman's voice.

6. English played backwards in the woman's voice (which, while quite incomprehensible, has the same content of voice frequencies as normal English).

7. A French translation of the English shadowed message in the woman's voice.

Table I shows the results of this experiment. If we compare 1 with 3 we can see that when the only acoustic cue available is the difference between the two ears, linguistic cues are not very successful in segregating the message to be

TABLE I
Irrelevant Message

	1	2	3	4	5	6	7
Average error	26	69	60	58	50	48	54

shadowed. (Other experiments, in which both messages are put into both ears, show that the task of shadowing becomes virtually impossible when this last cue of ear-difference is removed.) Introduction of the voice-difference decreases the error-score from 89 to 26 per cent—an improvement of nearly 115 per cent. Secondly, we may notice that even though the rejected message may be quite unavailable to the conscious memory of the subject, its character still has an effect on the filtering. Thus, for example, the language of biochemistry was much less familiar to these subjects than was that of an ordinary novel, and interfered appreciably less. The effect of the rejected message being in a foreign language was broadly to make the filtering process even more effective and the advantage was the greater the less familiar the subjects were with the language in question.

Perhaps oddly, the use of a French translation of the message to be shadowed did not, even for those who knew a great deal of French, make any appreciable difference. (Some of them did, indeed, become aware of the identity of the two passages and every now and then their shadowed versions contained elements clearly derived from the French.) The use of Czech pronounced in English phonemes proved about as distracting as any other foreign language with which the subject was not familiar. This seems to show that the efficiency of the whole filtering system is dependent on some relation between the parts concerned with sounds and those concerned with sense. Finally, the experiment using reversed English showed a slightly lower performance than that using Czech, a result which could perhaps be attributed to the attention-getting novelty of the sounds produced by reversal.

There may be nothing tremendously surprising in experimental results such as these. But taken altogether in conjunction with other observations they allow us to frame provisional theories or models of the filtering system, though we cannot go into these here. Such models allow more decisive experiments to be carried out. It is one thing to *expect* a result and another to *know* that it has been obtained, and to attach relative *quantitative* estimations to the various factors.

Another approach is to vary not the *rejected* message but the one which has to be *shadowed*. Following the general idea that the linguistic filter must operate at least partly in terms of the unequal probabilities of different words occurring in a given place (which should allow some degree of prediction or of replacement if they pass unheard), the subjects are made to shadow what have come to be known as 'statistical approximations' to ordinary language. These are not passages which are produced by a speaker who has something to say, but are generated by a procedure which allows them to be built up roughly according to probabilities governing the choice of words following a given word sequence. Thus, for example, I might construct a passage by simply drawing each successive word at random out of the dictionary. This, of course, generates nonsense, but the outcome is noticeably less nonsensical if I draw the words, not at random but in accordance with their relative frequency of occurrence in large samples of normal text. (Word lists giving these frequencies are available.) This is the kind of thing one gets:

> Representing and speedily is an good apt or come can different natural here he the a in came the to of to expert gray come to furnishes the line message had be these.

The next step is to choose each word in accordance with the probability that it will occur following the preceding word, or the preceding two, or three, words and so forth. The results are known respectively as *second, third, fourth orders of approximation*. Obviously no tables have ever been prepared which enable us to do this but a useful, if rough and ready, method is to get people to play a game rather like 'Consequences'. One person is given a strip of paper at the top of which are written, for example, the first three words of a sentence chosen by the experimenter. The first player's task is to think of a sentence of which these are the first three words, write down the fourth word, fold back the first word so that it cannot be seen and hand the paper on to the second player who repeats the process. Here is part of a sixth order approximation:

> I have a few little facts here to test need lots of time for studying and praying for guidance in living according to common ideas as illustrated by the painting which is hanging on our most precious line.

The passages have a certain charm and people have sometimes failed to distinguish them from the works of our more advanced prose writers. They read as if they are always just getting around to saying something definite, but constantly change the subject just before they do. Ophelia's talk was rather like this.

But the usefulness of passages such as these in experiments is that they represent different degrees of *unexpectedness* and these degrees can be estimated, if only relatively, on a numerical scale. To do this we get people to play another game. In this they are given the passages with some words—perhaps every fifth—missing and asked to guess what these are. By getting guesses from a lot of people we can estimate the uncertainty of each missing word in terms of the proportion of people who guess it correctly, for they will draw on their own implicit knowledge or sense of the probabilities of words occurring in the given context. It is thus possible to get an estimate of what is called the *amount of information* per word. And it is found that this measure bears a quite simple linear relationship to the *logarithm of the order of approximation*.

The term *information* is used in a technical sense, one which can be mathematically manipulated, and it means the amount of uncertainty which is resolved in the circumstances by knowing, as opposed to not knowing, which word *actually* occurs. The 'Theory of Information' forms one very important basis for the study of language and communication, and its development some twenty years back by C. E. Shannon and N. Wiener stimulated an immense amount of research. The reader who is sufficiently interested must be referred to other books mentioned in the list at the end of this chapter. But for our present purposes we must notice that the word *information* has only a rather paradoxical connexion with its more usual senses. A phrase which is so familiar to us that, having heard the first word or two, we can run off the rest for ourselves, lacks unexpectedness and in this sense conveys little information since we can know with considerable probability what was said without having actually heard very much of it. Such a phrase is described as *redundant*, again a technical term which means roughly the opposite of *information*. To convey anything much—to resolve a reasonable amount of uncertainty in the hearer—the speaker must say something which is to some degree unexpected. Of course, if he says anything as unexpected as the second order approximation quoted above, he won't convey anything much either, but in the technical sense he transmits a lot of information with each word. If the word sequence is chosen wholly at random the information per word is limited only by the total number of words in the language.

Now a lot of psychological experiments suggest that the brain can only process information (in this technical sense) at up to a certain maximum rate. The act of shadowing certainly demands processing of the information in the message, so it is a reasonable prediction that the accuracy of performance will fall off as the information content per

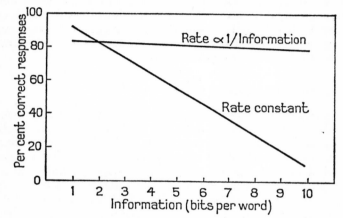

Fig. 5 'Shadowing' speech of varying information rates. (Based on data in A. M. Treisman, 'Attention and Speech', D.Phil. Thesis, Oxford, 1961)

word increases with falling order of approximation. When this experiment is done the prediction is borne out, as can be seen in Figure 5. We can clinch this by taking account of the fact that it is the *rate* of information processing which controls the performance (for all the messages were read at a standard number of words per minute). We should expect, therefore, that if the rate in words per minute is diminished in inverse proportion to the information content per word, the information *rate* being thus held constant, there should be no effect on performance. That this is very nearly true is shown by the top graph in the figure which is nearly parallel to the x axis.

Experiments like these—and many such have been done —allow useful models of the filter to be built up. By further experiment suggested by the model we can get progressively better insight into how we pay attention to one course of events to the temporary exclusion of all the other stimuli which constantly bombard us. Indeed, it is hardly too much to say that that hoary old psychological concept *attention*, which seemed to have been trampled down by the march of science, has staged a remarkable comeback through an engineer's practical concern with the factors which control ease of telephonic communication.

How Children Learn to Speak

The problem of how children can acquire language has been studied and speculated about for many years, on the whole with disappointing results so far as any basic understanding of it is concerned. But it happens that just at present a great deal of work in the psychology of language generally has to do with the mechanisms underlying its *grammatical* and *syntactical* aspects. These problems had been quite unduly neglected in the past, but contemporary grammatical theories and formulations such as those of N. Chomsky have had a powerful influence on research. Previous views about how meaningful strings of words are generated by the speaker and understood by the hearer tended to be based on the theory of information according to which each word has a certain probability of occurrence following the preceding words. And this seemed to tally reasonably with a conditioned reflex kind of view about the succession of items in behaviour generally. But the possession of an intuitive structure of probabilities about word sequences can hardly explain our capacity to understand sentences. For by playing such tricks as enclosing relative clauses repeatedly within one another, it is quite possible in principle to generate an unlimited number of different meaningful sentences. This means that nobody can have had the chance of building up knowledge of the probability structure of *all* the sentences he can understand. So we have to suppose that what the infant acquires is rather something in the nature of linguistic 'competence'. This means that he possesses intuitive knowledge, not of an immensely complicated scheme of probability structure relating to *particular words* but a grasp of general rules or laws which are independent of them. This system of rules has a hierarchical structure, so that two sentences such as *'John is easy to please'* and *'John is eager to please'*, which look superficially as if they were grammatically identical, can only be shown to be different by analysis of their *deep* structure.

Now one remarkable feature of the child's acquisition of his mother tongue is the very short time-interval between the stage at which he produces only two word sentences and that at which he is capable of all ordinary sentence production. The former stage is reached at about eighteen months: the latter at about five years. Moreover, it is evident that his first sentence utterances could not be analysed in any terms derived from adult grammar. This does not mean that the earliest, two word, sentences are *devoid* of regular structure, and a number of workers have devoted themselves to collecting specimens in the hope of finding out what their structure is, and tracing its evolution towards the adult form. At eighteen months the child has only a small vocabulary—though this is increasing rapidly—and it is possible to classify all the child's words according to the combinations into which they enter with other words. It seems that at first words fall into two classes, one a restricted class which may be called 'pivot' words. The other class could be called 'open', for it contains many items and these are being added to day by day. Each utterance consists of a pivot word followed by an open class word, and generally it seems that *any* pivot word could be so followed by any from the open class. Combinations of two pivot words, of two open class words or of an open class *followed* by a pivot have not been observed. On the whole the distinction between the two classes does not tally with adult grammatical categories such as parts of speech, though possessive pronouns and articles were found among the pivot class while nouns form the major part of the open class. Adjectives, however, might occur in either class.

We might say that the child does have a *kind* of grammar in its two word sentences, though this is quite different from that deployed by the adult. The next question is, obviously, how on earth does the one develop into the other? To trace this development completely will require vastly more observation and analysis than has yet been done. But a little progress has been made so far as the earliest stages are concerned. It seems that the first thing to happen is that the pivot class splits up into three parts, two of which approximate to adult categories. These are *articles* (*a, the*) and *demonstratives* such as *this* and *that*. At the same time rules develop to control the order of these two in the sentence, the demonstrative always coming before the article, followed by an item drawn from the new, restricted, pivot class and finally by a member of the open class. At the next stage the new pivotal class again splits into three parts, and adjectives and possessive pronouns become separated from the remainder of the class. New rules take the place of the older ones and these not only allow greater flexibility and variety in sentence construction, but produce sentences more nearly akin to adult forms though they still generally lack a verb. And, curiously, adjectives can have a place before *or* after a noun.

This work illustrates what it is reasonable to regard as an entirely fresh approach to the problem of language development. Previously workers thought almost wholly in terms of adult grammar and tended to confine themselves to such questions as that of the stages at which different parts of speech occurred, and were correctly used. There was little attempt to start with the child's speech itself and try to discover what structure it displayed. The new approach is a striking example of the stimulus which recent developments in pure linguistics have given to the empirical study of language behaviour generally.

What's In a Name?

Another pair of workers are engaged in what may seem at first sight a rather odd activity, that of measuring the *time taken to name an ordinary object*. The background to this research was roughly as follows:

One of the most common of the difficulties experienced by people whose speech and language have been disturbed by damage or injury to their brains is that of finding particular words. One may, indeed, well ask how the normal person does this at the speed most people ordinarily talk. This is at the rate of about two words a second and the speaker has at his disposal a very great many words out of which he must choose the right one at each moment. It is difficult to avoid the idea that the words—or rather some coded version of them—are somehow stored in the brain. The question then arises as to how the right word is searched for and retrieved. The problem is rather like that of how a particular book is found in a library. It would not be much good, for instance, looking at each word separately one after another until the one that fits is found, for this would take far too long. There must be some kind of classifying and indexing system, and the searcher must be able to use this. This means going through some sort of procedure by steps so that more and more words are eliminated at each. An example of such a step-by-step process is the use of a botanical key. To find the names of some flowers we have to go much farther through the key than for others, and this is because of the classifying system, which happens in this instance to be based on morphological features. In some ways this is not a very convenient arrangement, for it may often happen that a relatively common flower needs a lot of steps to find it while a much rarer one is to be found near the top of the tree. Now supposing each step to take a standard length of time, we might perhaps get an idea of the organisation and indexing system of the word store by finding out how long different sorts of words take to find.

Of course we don't very often need to find single words, and it is pretty clear that in ordinary speech the number of words that really come into question as possibilities at any given moment is very much limited by the context and the preceding series of words. The individual whose speech is disordered by brain damage (these disorders are known collectively as *aphasia*) can, indeed, sometimes find words very well once he gets started, so that the context, grammatical structure and so forth help him. Where he finds great difficulty is in finding *words in isolation*. One way to make him try to do this is to ask him the names of objects. It is, in fact, surprising to see a patient whose speech has almost completely recovered, and who might pass for normal in ordinary conversation fail to give the names of such common objects as a fountain pen or a pair of scissors, and this is a simple test for residual aphasia very commonly used by doctors. One thing seems clear, however, and this is that these names do not seem to be absolutely lost like a book stolen from a library. What seems to be at fault is the retrieval process, for the name may often be quite available in an ordinary sentence, while it cannot be produced in answer to the question, 'What is this?' Now some years back Williams and Rochford found that some names are consistently more difficult for the aphasic than others, and they found, too, that very much the same order applies to the ages at which children could first name the objects in question, to the performance of children at a given age, to the difficulty experienced by patients without brain damage but who were in a befuddled state following electric shock treatment, and to normal people who were distracted by a barrage of words which included wrong names. This raises the question of what it is that makes one name or one object more difficult than another, and this was tackled in an experiment on normal people.

Pictures of objects were shown to people who were instructed to produce the name as quickly as possible, but without making mistakes. The time this took was measured. These objects were so chosen that the frequency with which their names occur in the English language varied from pretty rare to pretty common. (This does not, of course, mean that the objects themselves are encountered in everyday life with the same relative frequencies.) The results of this experiment are quite clear as can be seen in Figure 6. There is a simple linear relationship between the reaction times and the logarithm of the frequencies. We cannot go straight from this result to any very specific hypothesis about the search

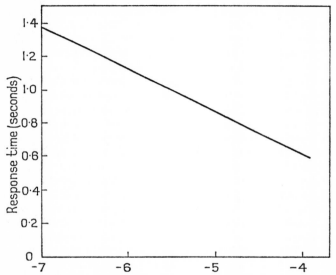

Fig. 6 Relation between text frequency of object-names and the time taken to produce them.
(Based on R. C. Oldfield and A. Wingfield, *Nature*, 1964, *202*, 1031)

process. But if the notion of a store applies at all to names we can at least eliminate certain types of organisation. A 'random-access' store—like the ones commonly used in computers—in which there is no kind of organisation, makes the average search-time the same for all the items. The most economical kind of organisation, on the other hand—that in which one decision eliminates half the items, the next half the remainder and so on—again results in equal times for all the items. In our word store, however, it is the commoner items which are the more quickly and easily retrieved, while the rarer take longer. So we are, perhaps, a little farther forward.

But this experiment itself on the whole raises more problems than it solves. One very awkward question is that of the proportion of the total time which is taken up in *recognising* or *identifying* the object, as opposed to searching for and finding the name. We can't attack this problem head-on because in general the only evidence one can get that somebody has identified something is his ability to put a name to it. However, quite a lot of further experiments have been done about this, none of which are entirely satisfactory. But the general outcome is to suggest that, in a normal person, the identification time is relatively brief, and only very little dependent on name-frequency. The frequency effect seems to be tied up with the *verbal* part of the search.

The people who did this experiment now got a clinical psychologist to collaborate with them. She did a very similar, if slightly simpler, experiment on quite a large number of people who had suffered injuries to their brains during the war. Some of them had disorders of speech and language, others not. In some the injury was to the left, or 'dominant' side of the brain, where the parts responsible for language functions are generally supposed to be situated, while in others the injury was to the right half. The left-sided group was divided into two, those with obvious signs of aphasia and those without. It can be seen from Figure 7 that measuring the times taken in this task does distinguish between the four groups. (Merely recording success or failure, as is usually done, does not.) The interesting point is that both the groups without aphasia but with injuries to their brains turn out consistently slower than the normal controls. Indeed, those with lesions in the right, 'non-dominant' side of the brain, are worse than those in whom the damage is to the left half. There may be many reasons for this. For instance, it might be suggested that anybody who has any damage to his brain may be a little slower in *all* his reactions than someone without such damage. But other tests of performance in these patients do not bear this out. The marked inferiority of those with right-sided damage presents in any case a point of special interest. It could, at least partly, be due to the difficulty which such patients are known to have

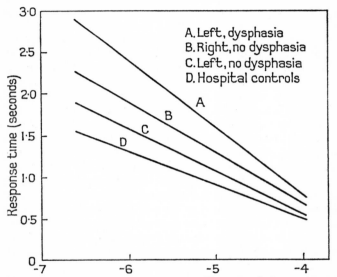

Fig. 7 Reaction times for naming by brain-injured people. (Based on data of F. Newcombe, R. C. Oldfield and A. Wingfield, in R. C. Oldfield, *Things, Words and the Brain*, Cambridge: Heffer, 1966)

in interpreting pictures. But it might also indicate, as has sometimes been suggested on other grounds, that the right half of the brain does, in fact, subserve some function concerned with language, even though damage to it does not reveal any evidence of this on ordinary clinical testing.

These language disorders in the brain injured are notoriously baffling and difficult to investigate. But it does seem as if progress will depend on more precise and quantitative methods being applied, and this piece of research at least illustrates how by combined work in the laboratory and the hospital clinic it may be possible to make a useful start with this.

Some Other Fields of Work

All this represents only a very small part of the mass of research which is going on nowadays, particularly in the United States. Many workers, for example, are investigating verbal learning and memory, while others are studying the ways in which one word calls up another by association. A good deal of attention has been paid to actual speech itself as it is used in everyday life, and the emphasis here is not so much on the strictly phonetic aspects but on such questions as that of *timing*. Why, and when, for instance, do pauses occur? How are gestures and other bits of non-verbal behaviour related to the speech they accompany? Social psychologists are now much interested in the different ways in which speech communication is used in different social circumstances and social groups. A great deal of effort is being put into the study of disorders of speech and language other than those due to brain disease. Some children are afflicted with stammering, others with what seems to be an inborn incapacity to read words, or to spell them. Children of very low intelligence, too, suffer from failure to develop fully this or that aspect of speech and language. Lastly, there has been a great renewal since the war of interest in the ways in which animals communicate and this has been helped forward by the availability of electronic equipment. The sounds made by fish, dolphins, birds and insects can now be recorded and a start has been made in sorting out the form their communication takes. With progress in all these fields the time may come when we shall have a very much clearer picture of how man first came to acquire the power of speech, and of the mechanisms which now subserve it in ourselves.

Opportunities

The moment when one is just about to become a university student is probably not the best for deciding exactly what one's final line of interest is going to be. Nevertheless, people do quite often find themselves handicapped through not knowing early enough just what they ought to do to get the opportunities they want. So it is perhaps worth while to say a word about this problem in relation to the field of speech and communication.

It is a new field and up to now only one first degree course (that at Newcastle) is designed to cover it, though students of Psychology will often find some aspects of the subject fairly fully treated, either as part of their general course or as an optional paper. The second thing to be said is that, as usual at a growing point, people of widely varying backgrounds are welcome. A *real* interest in, and feeling for, language is the first essential, and some reasonable knowledge of a foreign tongue or two a great advantage. Quite a lot of people come along who specialised in languages at school and now find themselves curious about what goes on in the human individual when he speaks, writes, reads or understands. But knowledge and competence in a linguistic discipline is not enough. People who want to make a scientific study of language processes need other skills, though the choice of these is fairly wide. Mathematics is an excellent starting-point, and working competence in the elementary parts indispensable. Physics is a good alternative, partly because the physical aspect of communication processes can rarely be neglected, and partly on account of the experimental and mathematical skills it teaches. A biological background is perhaps most favourable of all, for the study of speech and communication is moving fairly quickly into consideration of the actual processes in the nervous system which are involved.

When it comes to a university course there is, of course, the possibility of choosing psychology. On paper, at least, this would seem to have almost everything to be said for it. It is the only university subject which gives any substantial introduction to the problems we have been talking about. It gives a background grasp of what is known about other aspects of human behaviour, some of which are highly relevant to communicational processes. It provides opportunities to acquire experimental and other scientific skills. But it should be emphasised that work in the field of language and communication is many-faceted, with potentialities for future development which no one can predict with certainty. For a considerable time at any rate there will be scope for people who come from backgrounds as varied as linguistics to neurophysiology.

Armed, then, with a first degree in some relevant discipline, where does the would-be worker in this field go next? First it must be said that for the present his outlet is likely to be in research. The gateway to this is, for all practical purposes nowadays, a Ph.D., and there are a number of places where there are opportunities for doing this. Several university Departments of Psychology have a special interest in the subject, and resources for research and its supervision. Among these might be mentioned University College and Birkbeck College, London, Oxford, Edinburgh and Manchester. Keele is unique in having a Department of Communication which is active particularly in the fundamental problems, especially those of processes in the nervous system. Among research institutions the Medical Research Council's Applied Psychology Research Unit at Cambridge and its Speech and Communication Research Unit at Edinburgh encourage graduate students interested in this field. Two University Departments of Phonetics, those at University College, London, and Edinburgh, are engaged in work which has to do with the psychological as opposed to the purely acoustic features of speech, and several neurological clinics, for instance those at the National Hospital for Nervous Diseases, London, and the Churchill Hospital, Oxford, have psychologists working on the pathology of language.

It is, however, in the United States that by far the largest number of opportunities occur. The universities and other institutions where research into speech and communication in one form or another is going on are far too many for detailed mention. But information about these can always be got from the appropriate staff members of the British departments mentioned above.

Suggested Reading

Little, unfortunately, has yet been written for the non-specialist or beginner that describes recent developments, and much is still contained only in scientific journals. But the keen student may, according to his interests and background, find some of the following useful:

MILLER, G. A., *Language and Communication*, New York: McGraw-Hill, 1951.

Though written over fifteen years ago, this still provides a good introduction. Certain aspects, however, such as the part played by contemporary theories of grammar, and the cerebral mechanisms of speech, do not figure.

CHERRY, C., *On Human Communication*, Cambridge, Mass: M.I.T. Press (2nd edn.), 1966.

A vigorous and stimulating discussion ranging over a wide field from the physics to the psychology of communication, by an electrical engineer.

PIERCE, J. R., *Symbols, Signals and Noise*, New York: Harper, 1961.

A good introduction to the Theory of Information which will appeal most to those with a little physics and mathematics.

BROADBENT, D. E., *Perception and Communication*, Oxford: Pergamon Press, 1958.

Includes an experimental and theoretical account of message filtering mechanisms.

SMITH, F. and MILLER, G. A. (eds.), *The Genesis of Language*, Cambridge, Mass: M.I.T. Press, 1966.

Only browsing in this rather heavy work is recommended, but it gives an idea of the stimulus to the study of speech development provided by modern theories of grammar and syntax.

DE REUCK, A.V.S., and O'CONNOR, M. (eds.), *Disorders of Speech*, CIBA Foundation Symposium, London: Churchill, 1964.

Not intended as an introduction, but includes discussions by neurologists, psychologists, linguists and communication engineers, which illustrate contemporary research trends.

MARSHALL, J. and OLDFIELD, R. C. (eds.), *Readings in the Psychology of Language*, Harmondsworth: Penguin Books (in preparation).

Intended chiefly for undergraduate students of psychology; this represents an attempt to introduce the reader to some of the more recent research trends.

It will be worth the student's while to look through the journal *Language and Speech* which publishes a considerable variety of research reports covering a large part of our field.

6

Social Behaviour

Gustav Jahoda

Introduction

The field of social behaviour is wide, covering behaviour
influencing, influenced by, and related to, other individuals.
As such, one takes it for granted as part of the texture of
one's life, and does not think of it as a separate subject for
systematic study. Hence in order to acquire a suitable perspective it might be best to begin with a look at social
behaviour in animals. These have long been held up as
mirrors by philosophers and moralists who chose a tactful
way of showing up human foibles and follies, but the serious
study of animal behaviour dates back barely half a century.
Thus today the expression 'peck order' has become a conven-
tional phrase, but in 1920 the observations of Schjelderup-
Ebbe on social dominance in hens were a fresh discovery. He
undertook his studies in the seemingly unpromising setting
of the poultry yard. Many people must have looked at their
fowl over the centuries without making any sense of the
birds' apparently haphazard behaviour and occasional fights,
except to notice that the cock usually lorded it over the hens.
Schjelderup-Ebbe watched the inhabitants of the poultry-
yard over a period with the explicit question in mind: do
regular patterns of relation exist among individual hens?
He did find a rudimentary social organisation, established
after a period of fighting and thereafter relatively stable.
Each bird has its position in a dominance hierarchy, and this
probably serves the function of ensuring that physical conflict does not flare up every time food becomes available.
Schjelderup-Ebbe has some amusing comments about the

way in which birds low in the hierarchy seem to vent their spleen furiously on those lower still, while those high in the peck order are more 'reasonable'. It is tempting to apply this to human social behaviour: the corporal roars at the private, while the captain voices his commands to the corporal in crisp yet restrained tones. However, the temptation should be resisted; human social behaviour is vastly more complex, or else the dictator would be the most reasonable of men.

Since the Second World War there has been a great development of work on animal behaviour in relation to their normal living conditions. Ethology, as this study is called, differs radically from the laboratory investigations of animal psychologists, who place the animals in situations they are never likely to encounter in their natural habitat. This is, of course, no criticism of animal psychologists, since their aim is to study the laws governing such basic processes as perception and learning; for this purpose they expose the animals to a highly controlled environment which does not normally include other members of the same species. Consequently, they have not contributed a great deal to our understanding of social behaviour, and have sometimes even been led to draw false conclusions. It has, for instance, been said of rats, the species most intensively studied by psychologists, that they have 'very little social life'; in fact, the work of A. S. Barnett shows this to be a mistaken notion, and writers such as Lorenz and Tinbergen have described the social behaviour of a variety of species. None the less, it is true that social behaviour is a far less prominent characteristic of, say, rats or pigeons than it is of human beings or the social insects. The most highly socialised of the latter such as ants, termites or bees form communities that in some respects closely resemble human societies. Some of the details of the behaviour of aggregates of ants and men are similar: if one looks down from a height on to one of the narrow streets of old Naples, bustling with figures carrying baskets, one is strongly reminded of ants jostling each other along their path. When Darwin described the behaviour of ants, he was led to do so in anthropomorphic terms:

When the nest is slightly disturbed, the slaves occasionally come out, and like their masters are much agitated and defend the nest; when the nest is much disturbed, and the larvae and pupae are exposed, the slaves work energetically together with their masters in carrying them away to a place of safety. Hence, it is clear that the slaves feel quite at home. (*Origin of the Species.*)

Closer study of insect communities, far from dispelling this sense of remote kinship, tends to reinforce it. Thus the huge pillar-shaped termite nests, equivalent to skyscrapers, compel admiration by their remarkable interior design. They contain fungus gardens to supply the inhabitants with protein; there is an air-conditioning system, and even 'sanitary installations' which preserve brood chambers and storage spaces from the dangers of infection. Entomologists cannot as yet fully explain how relatively humble organisms are capable of such feats of adaptation to their environment. It is clear, however, that the richly varied and (on casual observation) seemingly haphazard behaviour of individuals forms part of a larger and coherent pattern; without close co-operation between members of the species, such elaborate structures would be impossible to achieve. Perhaps one direct example of such social co-operation may be cited: the weaver ants make use of their larvae to construct a nest from leaves joined by threads of silk. They work in well-integrated teams, some pulling the edges of leaves into alignment, others carrying the larvae which secrete sticky threads serving to glue the leaves together. Such co-operation is not confined to nest building but extends to practically every activity throughout the life cycle, and particularly to caring for the brood.

One of the major elements which make such collective achievements possible, in human as well as insect societies, is efficient division of labour. The social insects have evolved a mode of specialisation whereby certain types of individuals are *physically* best fitted to perform particular tasks. Such castes of workers or soldiers (note how the terminology is derived from analogy with human society) are produced by differential feeding of the larvae, which then develop into individuals of distinctive physical characteristics. In some species, such as the honey bee, even the sex ratio is determined by the community itself. The whole process leads to a balanced relationship with the external environment. The result is a marvellous stability of social organisation, of a kind never found in human societies. Lest we be inclined to envy this, it is useful to remember that there is always a price to be paid. In this case the obverse of the medal is rigidity; there seems to have been very little evolutionary change over several geological eras. Certainly the ants trapped and preserved in Baltic amber, long before even hominids appeared upon the scene, look just like the ants we know today.

The Framework of Human Social Behaviour

Human society rests on an entirely different basis, namely *psychological* as opposed to physical differentiation, though both are brought about by the community. The two characteristics of the human organism which make this possible are, first, the lengthy period of development from birth to maturity in the course of which the organism can be 'programmed' in a wide variety of ways and, second, the human capacity for symbolic communication by means of language. Insects are not altogether devoid of the latter, and bees in particular are able to indicate sources of food to their fellows by means of a dance 'language'; but at best this capacity remains severely restricted among insects. Human beings undergo an extensive process of learning, in the course of which the accumulated skills, knowledge and rules of behaviour are transmitted from one generation to the next. Animals are capable of this to a limited extent. For instance, a number of titmice must have independently discovered the trick of removing the tops of milk bottles, and this skill has probably been transmitted both within the same generation and also to the younger birds. In this manner adaptation to a vast range of different forms of social organisation becomes possible.

We must now turn to examine briefly some salient characteristics of human society, for this forms the framework within which human social behaviour takes place. Any human society is made up of an intricate network of social relations, usually called 'social structure'. These relations exist between individuals occupying particular positions, to each of which is attached a set of rights and obligations. As an example let us take the 'doctor', which word normally implies relations with another category of persons labelled 'patients'. The norms governing the behaviour of the occupant of any given position are called his 'social role'. Clearly an individual will usually fill several such positions simultaneously, and the doctor may also be a husband, a father or a church member. The behaviour of the individual will in the main be a function of the particular role he performs at the time; thus our doctor will conduct himself differently towards his patients, his wife, his children and his fellow church members. Moreover, the behaviour he adopts will not be arbitrary but laid down by society within certain limits. We can thus think of these positions in the abstract, as focal points for collections of rights and duties, involving certain forms of behaviour. In society the actual people manning the position do not remain the same; people die, and children are born and trained to take over the vacant positions. The element which alters more slowly is the basic pattern; but since human societies are far less rigid than insect ones the structure of society itself is subject to change, and over the past century its rate of change has vastly accelerated.

The analysis of social structure is the business of the social anthropologist and the sociologist, the former more frequently working in what are nowadays called 'developing' countries, the latter in advanced industrial societies. Anthropologists are on the whole more directly concerned with social behaviour, which is their raw material. Social structure is, of course, not something that can be directly observed. Radcliffe-Brown stated this very clearly:

Science (as distinguished from history or biography) is not concerned with the particular, the unique, but only with the general, with kinds, with events which recur. The actual relations of Tom, Dick and Harry or the behaviour of Jack and Jill may go down in our field note-books and may provide illustrations for a general description. But what we need for scientific purposes is an account of the form of the structure. For example, if in an Australian tribe I observe in a number of instances the behaviour towards one another of persons who stand in the relation of mother's brother and sister's son, it is in order that I may be able to record as precisely as possible the general form of this relationship, abstracted from the variations of particular instances, though taking account of these instances. (*Structure and Function in Primitive Society*.)

It is perhaps worth pointing out that Radcliffe-Brown does not use the expressions uncle and nephew, for the good reason that other cultures often make distinctions within the types of relations covered by our general terms. One of the main tasks of the field-worker is to sort out such distinctions in the context of actual behaviour: who greets and visits whom, who gives orders and who obeys, who shares meals with whom and so on. In addition to watching what they actually do, the field-worker also questions them in order to find out both what they say that they do, and what they feel they ought to do. In other words, he is interested in what the generally accepted ideal-type rules about social behaviour are, to what extent people feel obliged to claim that they actually follow these rules, and what kinds of departures from them are tolerated in practice. In our own society, for instance, honesty is acknowledged as an important norm that ought to govern social behaviour, and most people would claim that they adhere to it; in practice, however, petty swindling (e.g. of Customs) and 'white' lies of various kinds are not only extremely common but widely accepted.

On the basis of material collected in this manner the anthropologist constructs, as it were, a map of social behaviour from which certain principles may be derived. Thus it often turns out that kinship is a major key for the understanding of various forms of social behaviour; knowing a person's position in the kinship structure, it is possible to predict with considerable confidence how he is expected to behave in a wide variety of social situations. There are, of course, other organising principles, not necessarily mutually exclusive; for example, among the Konkomba in Northern Ghana an important one is the age-set, consisting of people born within a certain period:

> A man knows his place in his own set exactly; he knows the members of senior and junior sets and can therefore place himself relative to other sets. The principal function of the age-set system is to define seniority within the major lineage and it is seniority that decides who shall hold political and ritual office. (D. Tait, *The Konkomba of Northern Ghana.*)

It should be clear, therefore, that the anthropologist is generally not concerned with individual social behaviour as such, but uses it to build up a general picture of the social structure. The same applies also to the sociologist, whose work has been described in some detail in a previous volume. I may perhaps mention here that as he more often operates in a modern industrial society, his opportunities for the direct observation of social behaviour are generally less favourable. Much anthropological research is carried out in tropical or subtropical areas where a large part of social life takes place in the open. In colder climates, some of the most important facets of social behaviour, such as the interaction among members of a family, occur behind closed doors to which the sociologist has no access. This is a considerable handicap for both sociologists and social psychologists, especially since there are in western societies substantial differences between private and public behaviour. Goffman, a sociologist who has studied this difference and analysed it in dramaturgical terms emphasises the need people feel to present a public 'front'. The husband and wife who have just been locked in a furious quarrel will arrive at the party being very polite to each other (perhaps too polite, from which outsiders may guess the true state of affairs); the waiter who is brisk and efficient in serving the restaurant patron passes through the kitchen doors and is transformed into a weary man whose feet ache and who gives vent to his irritation at the capriciousness of the expense-account diners. The latter 'back-region' can, and has been, penetrated, while the former is almost completely inaccessible. Hence both sociologists and psychologists are often forced to resort to some form of questioning people about their social behaviour, and the answers are related to their actual social behaviour in a rather complex manner. On the other hand, as compared with the anthropologist, the sociologist has an advantage in having a great deal of documentary material available about such subsystems of the social structure as the economic, political, legal or religious.

Let us now sketch, for the sake of argument, a grotesquely oversimplified picture of a society: people behave in accordance with their social roles, which intermesh to keep the whole system going with reasonable smoothness. Anthropologists and sociologists have the task of mapping the system, but is there anything the psychologist can contribute? There are several answers to this question. In the first place, a social role is more like a trolley-bus than a tram; the general direction is determined, but considerable room for manoeuvre remains for people to enact a role in their particular style; the role of a schoolteacher, for instance, is fairly clearly defined; but within certain limits the teacher is free either to impose a harsh discipline on the children in his charge, or to encourage a great deal of free expression. There are thus wide individual differences in role behaviour, which are in the province of the psychologist. Secondly, the forms of conduct prescribed in any particular society exist only as a potential at birth, and the capacity to apprehend the nature of the society in which one lives develops only gradually. The stages in this development are an important subject of psychological study. Lastly, social norms and rules relate in the main to standard and repetitive situations; they save a great deal of time and effort, since there is no need for continuous choice and decision. This will be readily understood by anyone who has had the experience of moving into an unfamiliar social setting, perhaps merely for a holiday: at first situations that are trivial at home, such as shopping or getting a meal, are occasions for anxiety and stress because one is ignorant of 'the right thing to do'. However, outside such standard and recurring situations there is a vast area of social behaviour which is not governed by any explicit or implicit norms, though even this kind of behaviour exhibits regularity. Examples are the behaviour of people in small groups, the manner in which they form impressions of others or acquire prejudices which subsequently influence their behaviour. All these are grist for the psychologist's mill, and the outcome of his studies has practical relevance in such spheres as behaviour at work, race relations and delinquency. Some of these themes will now be taken up in more detail, beginning with the genesis of social behaviour in the individual.

The Development of Social Behaviour

There are a great many distinct though related questions that can be asked about this: how is a new-born infant, a screaming, helpless bundle, transformed into a socially mature adult member of human society? What are the effective differences in treatment that produce a Briton fitting into British society rather than a Frenchman, Russian or Nigerian? What are the stages in the child's development of an intellectual awareness of his social environment? What are the factors, both internal and external, which shape his conduct increasingly in accordance with social rules and norms, or in some instances fail to do so? Without any pretensions to be systematic, some of these topics will be surveyed so as to illustrate both the range of problems studied and the methods employed.

The new-born infant cannot be said to exhibit any form of behaviour that might strictly be called 'social'. The earliest trace of response to social stimulation has been detected at four weeks. During the second month the smile appears, and this is the first truly social behaviour. The mother who bends over her baby's cot and is rewarded with the first smile will feel with delight that she has established real person-to-person contact with her offspring. Alas for this touching scene—at this early stage she is almost certainly mistaken. What are the grounds for saying so, and by what means has it been demonstrated?

The trick, as in most significant advances was, first, to question something generally taken for granted and, secondly, to devise means for testing certain hunches. In this particular instance the classical work was undertaken by Spitz, who questioned whether it was the actual presence of a live human being that made the infant smile. He conducted experiments with several hundred infants from various ethnic groups and living in different types of environment (e.g. at home or in institutions), so as to ensure that his conclusions would not be confined to any particular subgroup. The actual procedure consisted in the main of presenting infants with systematically varying stimuli, which enabled him to ascertain which specific characteristics of the stimulus were effective in eliciting a smile. It turned out that with the youngest infants a considerable range of stimuli were effective, including, for instance, a Hallowe'en mask. Later it was shown by Ahrens that the mere crude representation of eyes by two black dots below the outline of the top half of a head was enough to produce a smile up to the age of about three months. With such young infants, and using more elaborate representations of the human face, the expression depicted was immaterial; in other words, a horrifying mask is just as good as a friendly and cheerful one for making the infant smile. At this stage, therefore, the infant is totally incapable of reading emotional attitudes from faces. Similarly, infants below five months cannot discriminate between familiar persons and strangers, smiling at anyone who approaches them. Thereafter a change occurs, and by about eight months not only are smiles confined to familiar faces but strange ones may begin to arouse fear. At roughly the same period, infants begin to be able to form attachments to specific individuals, so that their social behaviour ceases to be indiscriminate.

At this point two comments are appropriate. First, some of the research just described is not merely of theoretical interest: it has a bearing on the problem of the age at which children may safely be separated from their mothers when treatment in hospital is needed. Secondly, it is worth noting that the methods used in studying social behaviour before the emergence of language closely resemble some of those employed by ethologists when investigating the behaviour of animals. Thus in order to discover what are the necessary and sufficient stimuli to 'release' aggressive behaviour in certain species of fish, dummies varying in shape, size and colour are presented until aggression is regularly produced; or again, the 'gaping response' of nestling thrushes is normally associated with parent birds approaching with food; but it can be elicited by a stimulus conforming to the following specifications: it must move; it must be larger than 3 mm in diameter, and it must be above the horizontal plane passing through the nestlings' eyes (Tinbergen).

From all this an important moral can be drawn: the determinants of social (and, of course, other forms) of behaviour are not necessarily those which appear obvious to the hard-headed no-nonsense bystander who believes firmly in common sense. Another illustration of this may be provided from child behaviour. It has long been taken as axiomatic that praise and approval from adults is an effective 'reinforcement' (i.e. means of increasing the strength and/or frequency of a particular response) with children. In recent years systematic studies of the effectiveness of this kind of social reinforcement indicate that it is in reality very complex, varying widely under different conditions; and we are far from fully understanding it. Such experiments can, of course, only be conducted from the age of about three onward, when children have acquired the ability to interpret the behaviour and expression of people in their environment. The tendency for the characteristics of people to become increasingly important with advancing age was demonstrated in an ingenious series of investigations by Levy-Schoen;[1] an example of one of these will be given. Children between the ages of four and thirteen were shown pairs of pictures, and asked which they preferred. The first choice was between toys—an aeroplane and a football; the second between a smiling and a frowning boy. The last and crucial choice depended on the outcome of the previous ones; suppose the child had preferred the football and the smiling boy; in that case he was shown a smiling boy holding an aeroplane, and a frowning boy holding a football. In other words, preferences for physical objects were pitted against those for characteristics of people.

The outcome can be seen in Figure 1, where the choices of each age group are plotted. Until about seven years 'toy'-

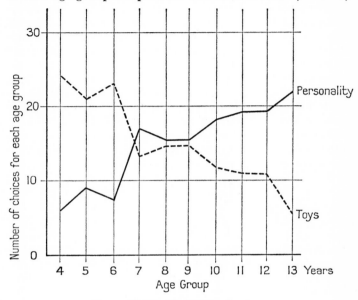

Fig. 1 Children's Choices by Ages

choices greatly predominate, and after nine years give way to the 'personality' ones.

At the same time as children learn to become more sensitive and discriminating in their orientation to other people, they also begin to learn the roles they are expected to play in their society. The most fundamental division here is that between the sexes. By the age of three, a majority of children know their own sex; during the two subsequent years they learn not only to identify that of others from bodily cues as well as clothing but they also get to know that different things are 'done' and 'not done' by boys and girls respectively. The most obvious models of sex division are, of course, the figures of mother and father in the family, and the child begins to distinguish their roles soon after their personal sex-identity is established. Incidentally, this identity is fostered by a variety of means, beginning with colour symbolism (pink versus blue), followed by distinctive clothing, different toys and the constant voicing of suitable sentiments by people in the child's environment ('Isn't he/she like his dad/her mum?') Behaviour towards other children also undergoes a gradual differentiation by sex. In studies of friendship choices it was found that at the age of five about a quarter of the friends are of the opposite sex; by ten years interests have diverged sufficiently to bring about the virtual disappearance of cross-sex choices. Changes of a similar kind, allowing for the radical contrast in cultural setting, occur in other societies. Thus Fortes decribes the pattern in a tribe of Northern Ghana:

> By the age of about nine or ten children begin to adopt the sexual division of labour customary among the Tallensi, and with it the corresponding division of social rôles and ideals. Boys start following their older brothers and take their turn at herding their father's cattle if he has any. They are becoming more skilful with the hoe and by the age of about twelve reach a high degree of proficiency ... A girl of nine or ten is learning from her mother how to cook, how to beat floors and plaster walls, how to carry out all the domestic duties of a housewife. She is acquiring the woman's view of life centred on marriage and motherhood. (*The Web of Kinship among the Tallensi.*)

Apart from sex roles, there are a great many others the child has to learn to understand if his social behaviour is to become appropriate to the norms of his society. As has already been indicated, social positions are commonly ranked hierarchically, being accorded varying degrees of prestige. The most extensive stratification, as this is often called, is to be found in India. There the so-called caste system used to be extraordinarily rigid, being maintained by religious sanctions. Castes consisted largely of occupational groups, and contact between them was severely restricted so as to avoid 'pollution'. At the bottom of the scale the 'untouchables' were to be found, regarded as unclean. The Indian constitution of 1950 removed the legal basis of untouchability, but it could not immediately alter the patterns of social behaviour. This is readily understood when one considers the manner in which the avoidance rules were stamped in during childhood. This was observed by Carstairs:

> As the child learned to accept responsibility for its own bodily cleanliness, it was also taught the importance of avoiding the invisible pollution conferred by the touch of members of the lower castes. The mother or grandmother would call him in, and make him bathe and change his clothes if this should happen, until his repugnance for a low-caste person's touch became as involuntary as his disgust for the smell and touch of faeces. (*The Twice-Born.*)

Compared with this, social stratification in Britain is very moderate; but this certainly does not mean that it is negligible. Sociologists and psychologists have studied this question extensively, showing that the social class of an individual affects educational opportunities quite apart from ability, is related to voting behaviour, choice of marriage partner and a variety of other forms of social behaviour. Since social class is of considerable importance in a person's life, one would expect that children growing up in our kind of society would have to learn about it. At the same time, a certain taboo still remains attached to this subject; children are not formally taught about it at school, and most parents would indignantly deny that they attempt any deliberate teaching. This is no doubt perfectly true, but a good deal of incidental learning must occur in many everyday situations when children have the opportunity of witnessing encounters between their parents and people of the same or other social class: behaviour towards, say, the milkman will differ at least in subtle ways from that towards the doctor. In this way children build up a notion of social class many years before they understand the term 'class'. This was established in an investigation using a form of puzzle where social class rather than physical fit is relevant. It will be readily understood from the example in Figure 2, where four pieces had to be put together in pairs. From six years onward children increasingly paired the figures according to social class, insisting that the other way round would be

Fig. 2 Example of the 'Puzzle' used by Social Class Conception Study. (From G. Jahoda, 'Development of the Perception of Social Differences in Children from 6 to 10', *British Journal of Psychology*, L, 2, 1959)

'wrong'; as one girl aged eight put it, 'You wouldn't like to shake hands with a workman, because their hands are dirty; it's much nicer the other way.' By the age of ten, a large majority of the children studied were able to complete the 'puzzles' correctly, though not necessarily to explain their reasons.

The answer given by the little girl was fairly typical (though most others were not quite so snobbish!) inasmuch as it indicated not only an awareness of differences but also of feelings attached to them. The same was found more recently when studying children's ideas of nationality, usually the largest social unit with which people identify and for which they are sometimes prepared to sacrifice their lives. Small children of six or seven lack any clear conception of a nation; even geographically, a term like 'England' remains vague in the extreme, and they are just as likely to say 'England is in London' as the converse. And yet, English children of that age on being told that some people are English and others not English will already tend to show a greater preference for those who have been described as English; similarly, on being asked to guess whether people they like are English or not English, they tend to plump for the former.

It will perhaps have been noticed that the focus of the discussion has quietly shifted. At the outset a rough sketch of the social world was drawn and, considering it as a kind of maze, we asked how children from infancy onwards gradually come to find their way around; in other words, we began with the cognitive aspects. Latterly, however, there was increasing reference to feelings and emotions. In practice, both aspects are closely interwoven; the child not only learns about his family, class and nation but also develops sentiments concerning them; he not only learns the rules and skills of social behaviour but also learns to become uncomfortable or guilty when he fails to conform to these rules or lacks the appropriate skills. This second kind of learning is a very complex and subtle process, and its nature remains the subject of some controversy. Curiously enough, interest in this problem area of emotion and personality preceded the interest in the more straightforward cognitive development. This was due to the powerful influence of Freud and of psychoanalytic theory, which maintains that the experiences of infancy and early childhood largely go to shape adult personality and character; modes of infant care, weaning (gradual or abrupt), toilet training (harsh or relaxed) and the general degree of indulgence or severity were held to be paramount factors in determining the characteristics of personality, and thereby the social behaviour, of adults. The next step, taken by such followers of Freud as Kardiner, was based on the observation that different societies and cultures varied widely in social structure and behaviour as well as in methods of child training. The extent of these contrasts may be illustrated by an example: in Britain weaning is usually gradual, and the mother maintains her interest and attention for the child after it is completed. In some other cultures the mother is completely indulgent with the child, carries it around on her back all the time and offers the breast whenever it cries —until another child is due. Then she may smear some hot pepper on her nipples so that the child is 'burnt' when trying to suck the breast; he is handed over to the care of others in the household, while the mother transfers her attention to the new-comer. If one believes at all in the importance of early childhood experiences, and there is ample evidence that it is important, then it is not unreasonable to assume that such radical differences will have their effects on later behaviour. Now since society is made up of a web of social relations, it was further argued that the people occupying the different positions in the social structure, and interacting in political, economic and religious institutions, will need to have certain personality characteristics in common if the society is to function effectively. Thus a link was postulated between child training, which 'involves the moulding of raw human nature' (Kluckhohn), adult personality and the social pattern. This idea proved attractive to social anthropologists (at least American ones—the British remained sceptical) and a great deal of joint research was undertaken by anthropologists, psychologists and psychiatrists. The outcome of all this has been a series of fascinating studies describing various cultures and conveying the feeling that one understands them. At the same time, no general principles have emerged that can be applied directly to other cultures as yet not investigated in this manner. Thus, let us suppose we have an account of adult social behaviour in a particular culture, for example, the Nyakusa described by Wilson. Much of their social behaviour can be accounted for in terms of their belief that the sexual activities of succeeding generations must be kept strictly apart, or else evil consequences will follow. From this flows an extraordinarily rigid taboo on any form of contact, direct or indirect, between father-in-law and daughter-in-law:

> A woman may never look at her father-in-law nor enter his house, nor meet him on the path, nor mention his name, or words like it. She avoids even the cow which looked into his grave, and the flesh of the cock which was in his homestead, and the banana grove where her husband prays to his dead father. (*African Systems of Marriage and Kinship*.)

Given an exhaustive knowledge of these and other characteristic behaviour patterns, could we infer the nature of child-rearing practices? Or, conversely, if we had adequate information on child rearing practices, the physical environment and the economy, could we infer the major aspects of adult behaviour? The answer, unfortunately, is 'no', since these relationships involve a multitude of highly complex factors which cannot be readily disentangled within any one culture.

In order to overcome this problem, a new approach has been devised which makes it possible to examine more restricted relationships over a wide variety of different cultures for which relevant information is available. An example will help to clarify the method. Whiting[2] elaborated an hypothesis (on theoretical grounds that need not concern us here) that degree of severity of child-rearing practices would be associated with fear of ghosts at funeral ceremonies. Now in any particular culture this relationship, even if valid, might be masked by all kinds of irrelevant circumstances; on the other hand, if there is anything in it, this should emerge from a comparison of a variety of cultures. The actual results from forty-five cultures are set out in the table below:

		Fear of Ghosts at Funeral Ceremonies	
		Low	High
Indulgence in	Low	8	12
child-rearing	High	20	5

It will be seen that high indulgence in childhood tends

to go together with low fear of ghosts, while severity and neglect are associated with the prevalence of such fears. The likelihood of such a finding being obtained by chance is low, hence the results are in accordance with the original hypothesis.

While this method makes use of existing data, another way is to reduce the vast problem of the relationship between culture and personality to more limited issues, amenable to direct study. This was done by McClelland who concentrated on one particular motive for social behaviour, which he labelled the 'achievement motive', and a discussion of it will be found in Emerson (see reading list).

Social Interaction

Until now the perspective has perhaps been somewhat lopsided. First, after a brief glance at animal behaviour, we looked at human society as through a telescope from a great distance, so that only the coarse outlines were visible; this may have given a misleading impression of simplicity, but at least it brought out the underlying structure which accounts for the regularities of social behaviour. Then we turned a microscope on the individual human infant and focused on certain limited aspects of the process whereby the individual gradually comes to fit into the structure. What has been missed out until now has been the way social behaviour looks to ordinary unaided vision; so let us try and fill in this part of the picture.

Imagine we are in a train, observing two men sitting on opposite sides of a compartment. At intervals they lift their heads up from their reading and scrutinise each other casually and unobtrusively, carefully avoiding any blatant staring. Then, on a few occasions, their glances meet momentarily. A little later one of them, whom we shall call Mr. A, deliberately seeks out the eyes of Mr. B and remarks that the compartment is not well-heated. B agrees, and complains more generally about the weather nowadays. Mr. A feels certain that it has been upset by nuclear tests. From this they go on to discuss the state of the world at large, returning after a while to the way this affects them individually. It transpires that both are in similar lines of business, and after some search ('do you by any chance happen to have come across X?') they discover a common acquaintance. At this point we leave them to their animated conversation, and go on to examine this very commonplace episode as a piece of social behaviour. For this purpose, we shall go over the sequence again, singling out certain features; and later some of these will be discussed in more detail.

First of all, the emphasis placed on the initial by-play involving mutual glances may have struck the reader as odd. In fact, this is a by no means unimportant mode of non- (and often, as in this example pre-) verbal communication. The meeting of glances, or 'eye contact' in technical terms, constitutes a tacit agreement that a social interchange can take place. The initial topic, or rather gambit, of conversation is apt to be an entirely neutral one; statements about temperature or weather convey hardly any information about the external world. What they do is to provide the participants with samples of each other's speech; and from the accent and vocabulary they obtain additional information about each other's position in society, their social status. It is additional, since they will previously have had the opportunity of appraising each other on the basis of their clothing standards, general bearing and manner, as well as, for example, the kind of newspaper they are reading. The whole process so far is not unlike two strange dogs sniffing one another, or even ants meeting on a path sensing each other with their feelers to find out if they come from the same nest. Thereafter the analogy breaks down, since human beings go on to explore the other person's cast of mind. Does he have similar views to my own about the state of the country and the reasons for it? Having established such consensus, it becomes safe to disclose more personal information about oneself, which may be taken as a sign of willingness to establish a less formal relationship. This becomes further strengthened if a social bond in the form of a common relation to a third person is discovered.

Note that at several stages there are choice points where the interaction might cease. At the outset, B could avoid A's glance, thereby indicating that he has no wish to be addressed. This brings out a fundamental characteristic of face-to-face relation between people: there is nearly always mutual interplay, with each actor anticipating the moves of his partner to some extent, and knowing that the partner is doing the same. In our present example B is well aware that A is 'looking for an opening'; B in turn actively eludes the pursuit, yet without seeming to do so deliberately, which might be construed as rudeness. Experienced waiters are usually highly skilled in preventing patrons from 'catching their eye' if they are busy. Returning to our situation, the second choice point occurs after a few generalities have been exchanged; if these first few speech samples are judged unsatisfactory by either (he sounds uncouth/snobbish), they may terminate the conversation at that stage. Later still they may discover that their views about the world and its ills, contrary to their expectation, diverge so radically that there is no common ground, and they relapse into silence.

This brief sketch should be enough to show that even a seemingly trivial social encounter constitutes in reality a fairly complex process, the elements of which have been extensively studied by sociologists and psychologists. A few of these will now be examined, beginning with the visual aspect of social interaction. The importance of this visual element, especially among people of the opposite sex, has not escaped the notice of writers and poets: 'Love's tongue is in the eyes.' The French sociologist Pierre Henri has commented on how the blind are deprived in this respect:

> The blind person, who can neither express his feelings or desires by a glance, nor above all read from the glances of others the tacit agreements or subtle indications of annoyance is ill equipped to play the rôle of a seducer. ... At the first stage of relations between the sexes only the visual mode of conveying information and expressing emotion is socially acceptable. (*Les Aveugles et la Société.*)

While several sociologists have considered this problem of visual interaction, it was mainly Goffman who attempted a more systematic treatment in one of his brilliant and insightful works (*Behavior in Public Places*). Thus he introduced the notion of 'civil inattention', by which he means an unformulated rule that in the company of strangers you allow your glances to stray sufficiently in their direction to signal your awareness of their presence, yet not so much as to suggest that they are a special object of curiosity. He adds that the closer two people are physically, the greater their feeling of obligation to accord the other 'civil inattention'; and anybody sharing a small lift, or travelling in the underground during the rush-hour can verify this.

A short digression is necessary here to explain that physical distance as such is an interesting variable in social behaviour. There is evidence that already among animal species there are characteristic distances between members of a group, which may range from zero among some kinds of monkeys who cling to each other to about two feet among flamingoes. Human cultures also exhibit considerable differences in this respect. An anthropologist (Hall) suggests that for Americans the comfortable distance for two people engaged in conversation is about the same as that of flamingoes, but for other cultures it is much closer; and he has an amusing account of 'Yankees' in Latin America trying to preserve the distance by means of barriers of tables and chairs, and the Latin Americans climbing over them so as to get close enough to be able to talk properly.

Sociologists and anthropologists have accumulated many interesting observations in naturalistic situations, but they generally remain at the descriptive level. Psychologists, on the other hand, prefer whenever possible to carry out their observations under controlled experimental conditions.

Part of such an experiment, conducted by Argyle,[3] will be outlined. Its theoretical background need not concern us in detail, but the rationale of his predictions, based on previous research, must be outlined. First of all it has been established that the duration of eye-contact increases with personal intimacy, and this particular factor was held constant—all the subjects were strangers meeting in the laboratory for the first time. He then predicted that there would be a direct relation between duration of glances and physical distance; in other words, eye-contact would diminish with greater proximity, and increase with greater distance. In this way there is a kind of moving equilibrium, whereby the same degree of intimacy in terms of glances is maintained.

In the actual experiment, subjects were asked jointly to make up a story about a picture, and each pair held three conversations at distances ranging from 2 to 10 ft. Unknown to the subjects, one member of each pair was a confederate of the experimenter who gazed continuously at the genuine subject. Observers were stationed behind a one-way mirror (a device for keeping them invisible) and recorded eye-contact. The results were in accordance with the prediction: average duration of glances was nearly twice as long at 10 ft as compared with 2 ft, and their frequency can be seen in Figure 3.

Apart from these emotional aspects of eye-contact, it also serves the purpose of communication. It has been shown that at the end of a speech people look at their interlocutors; this is likely to be for the purpose of discovering the effect of what they have said, and prepare the next move accordingly. It has also been argued that written language differs in its structure from direct oral communication because in the former case the meaning conveyed by facial expression is absent. For instance a critical comment, delivered in a friendly tone and with a reassuring smile is one thing, and the same remark written down is quite another; in order to avoid appearing offensive, it may have to be toned down and thus rendered more impersonal. This seems entirely plausible, but recent research in France[4] suggests that the issue is more complicated. Conversations were studied with pairs of speakers in four positions: (a) face to face; (b) back to back; (c) side by side, and forbidden to turn to each other; (d) positioned face to face, but separated by a screen. The speech produced under these four conditions was then analysed in terms of the extent to which it tended to resemble written language in character. According to the principle just discussed, the odd one out should be (*a*) since it is the only one where people were able to scan each others' faces.

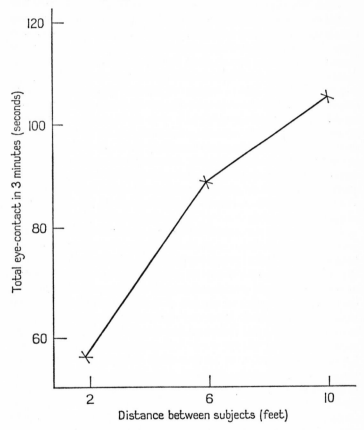

Fig. 3 Relation between Duration of Eye-Contact
and Distance

In fact, while it was confirmed that (*b*) and (*c*) approximated written language more, it turned out that (*d*) came closer to (*a*) than to (*b*) and (*c*). From this it was concluded that the nature of the social relation created by the situation determined the mode of speech more than the visibility or lack of it of the partner.

From here we return to our two men in the railway carriage, and take up another theme, the compatibility of their attitudes. It was said that their interaction might cease if they discovered that 'their views about the world and its ills, contrary to their expectation' diverge radically. Now attitudes may be somewhat crudely described as *dispositions* to respond favourably or unfavourably to particular objects, which might be, for example, types of people, institutions or social practices. Thus a person may have a favourable attitude towards public schools, the church, capital punishment and the Conservative party; another towards comprehensive schools, humanism, nuclear disarmament and the Labour party. These examples were not chosen at random but to indicate that attitudes tend to go together in clusters; this was documented in detail in the famous study on *The Authoritarian Personality*, discussed by Emerson. Attitudes are acquired in the course of an individual's life experience, and although these experiences vary extensively, it still remains true that people occupying similar positions in society tend to have more of these experiences in common than those in different positions. Consequently, we generally expect certain types of people to have appropriate kinds of attitude. Supposing, therefore, that our two characters both have the appearance of respectable and prosperous business men, it will be a shock for A to find that B is an ardent nuclear disarmer, and he may well decide that B is not a nice person to know.

In general, friendship patterns tend to develop among people with similar personality characteristics and attitudes, a fact already enshrined in proverbial wisdom—'Birds of a feather flock together'. Nevertheless, it would be rash to conclude that in this sphere psychologists and sociologists are labouring painfully to demonstrate the obvious. Quite apart from the fact that for most proverbs another one can be cited that contradicts it (e.g. 'Opposites attract each other'), it has been shown in studies of housing estates, for instance, that sheer physical proximity is an element pro-

moting frequent interaction and hence the formation of
social bonds. Which, if any, is the dominant factor? There
is probably no universal answer to this, but several researches
have thrown light on the question. Newcomb rented a
house and brought together sets of students who were initially total strangers to one another. In return for board and
lodging, and with ample freedom to run the place as they
thought fit, they agreed to take periodic tests and remain
under observation. The first patterns of relationship to
emerge were largely determined by the accidents of proximity, e.g. sharing a room. Common attitudes and interests,
assessed at the outset, contributed little to these early groupings; this is not surprising, since the students had not yet
had much opportunity of finding out about each other.
However, the original attitude measures predicted with
substantial accuracy the final groupings crystallised after a
period of four months. It is clear, therefore, that in this type
of situation proximity is secondary to a shared outlook.

What happens in another kind of situation where, after
people have come together as a group, they discover that
one of their number fails to share their attitudes on an issue
of importance to a majority of the members? There have
been several studies on this, showing that pressures come
to be exerted. In one of the best-known of these, made by
Schachter, groups interested in juvenile delinquency were
asked to discuss a bad character called 'Johnny Rocco' and
make recommendations as to what should be done with him.
The alternatives ranged from 'all-love' to 'all-punishment',
and since the case was presented in a manner suggesting that
Johnny had been a victim of circumstances, most of the
group members tended to cluster near the positive end of
the scale. However, unknown to the genuine group members,
the experimenter had in each case planted a stooge who
expressed views to the effect that a jolly good beating would
be the best thing. At first the discussion was fairly general,
but gradually as the discordant attitude of the 'deviant'
became manifest, more and more communications were
directed at him in an attempt to change his opinion and
bring him into line with the rest. Later still, when it became

evident that he would remain adamant, these efforts usually decreased. However, by then the group had effectively rejected him, as shown by a subsequent popularity vote.

So far, only the form of the interaction has been considered, irrespective of its content. We did not ask whether the views of the majority about 'Johnny Rocco' were more or less sensible than those of the deviate. Historically, it has been one of the main issues: are groups superior or inferior to individuals morally and intellectually? The German idealist philosophers took the former view, and most famous champion of the latter was the French writer Le Bon, who held that 'the crowd is always intellectually inferior to the isolated individual'; note that by 'crowd' he meant not only mobs but all kinds of organised interacting groups as well, such as parliaments or juries. The echoes of this dispute have not died down altogether. For instance, while Le Bon rather mildly remarked that criminal juries displayed 'but slight capacity for reasoning', a contemporary editorial writer (*New Society*, 5 May 1966) argued that lawyers would not permit evidence about what transpired in the jury room because 'inquiry would frequently reveal an intolerable tangle of prejudice and illogic'. In fact, the Chicago Law School has sponsored a Jury Project with the objective of studying the group pressures involved under as realistic conditions as possible (subjects drawn from an actual jurors' panel listened to a recorded trial and held their deliberations in the Jury Room of a Law Court); although the primary aim was not the assessment of the degree of rationality, there was no indication that the numerous groups of men and women behaved like bigoted half-wits.

As an illustration of the persistence of the opposite view, that groups are superior, one may take the practice of 'brain-storming'—not to be confused with brain-*washing*. This originated during the late 1930s in an advertising agency, and gained a tremendous vogue in the early postwar period. The basic notion is that if a group of people get together and are able to fire off ideas as they come into their heads, without fear of criticism or contradiction, a kind of chain reaction will ensue and produce a far greater

G U S T A V   J A H O D A

crop of creative ideas than individuals could think up by
themselves. This claim was subjected to a stringent experimental scrutiny by a team at Yale. A number of suitable
topics provided scope for bright ideas, e.g. how to attract
more European tourists. Subjects were allocated to two conditions, and since this is the crux of the method it will be
explained schematically. Supposing there are eight subjects,
labelled A to H; these are divided randomly into two sets,
as set out below:

ADEG   B C F H

Now *ADEG* were kept together as a real group and set to
brain-storming; the other four *B, C, F* and *H* were put to
work *individually* on the same problems, but the resulting
ideas were pooled afterwards. Therefore the results of this
latter 'nominal' group provide a standard of comparison. If
brain-storming is effective, it ought to yield more ideas than
the merely nominal group. The outcome was that the latter,
i.e. individuals working on their own, together produced
on the average nearly twice as many ideas as the brain-
storming groups.

One must be cautious, though, and not jump to conclusions. What we have learnt after a generation of work
in this field is that the opposition 'group *versus* individual'
is a misleading one. Being able to ask the right question is
half the battle; and as far as the interaction of people in
solving problems or producing ideas is concerned, we now
ask: under what conditions do particular types of groups
do better or worse at certain tasks, compared with specified
types of individuals? Contrasted with the simplicity of the
earlier question, this is perhaps rather clumsy; but unlike
the earlier question, it does at least make sense, and we do
have evidence for some of the answers.

The Study of Social Behaviour and Contemporary Problems

Much of the discussion so far may perhaps have conveyed
the impression that the study of social behaviour is largely
a theoretical exercise, not devoid of interest but remote

from everyday life. In reality, there are many fields of application; some are direct and may be called 'technological', the others are more remote, yet may prove ultimately to be of greater importance since they deal with fundamental issues.

One of the most widespread practical applications concerns problems of work, within the field of occupational psychology. This field as a whole covers a broad range including vocational guidance (advising people about their choice of occupation), personnel selection (choosing suitable people for particular jobs), industrial training, inspection, accidents and safety, physical working conditions. It was in a study of the last of these, a generation ago, that the effect of social factors forcibly obtruded itself. The aim was to study the effect of level of illumination on output; two groups of workers were selected to operate under closely similar conditions except that in the 'test' group illumination was systematically increased, while remaining constant in the 'control' group. Production did go up, but, contrary to all expectations, about equally in *both* groups. The wish to get to the bottom of this apparently strange outcome led to an ever-increasing interest in the social aspects of work behaviour. It was discovered that informal working groups often evolved a norm restricting output within certain limits, and that social pressures ranging from teasing to ostracism were exerted on those who failed to conform. Such norms were also found to be at the root of resistance to the introduction of innovations designed to increase productivity. It is often easier to diagnose the source of the trouble in a complex social situation than to find an effective remedy; and what seems to work in the short run does not necessarily solve the problem permanently. Thus one study, still extensively quoted, dealing with obstacles to industrial change in a pyjama factory claims to have overcome the difficulties by encouraging workers to participate in discussions about the change, and output was in fact maintained. What is not usually reported is the further development: the workers continued to discuss after the researchers had left, and decided that the whole procedure had been a device to exploit them more thoroughly; consequently they joined the union! In fairness it ought to be explained that this happened at a time when the so-called 'human relations' approach was apt to be regarded by managers as a useful means of manipulating, or at least influencing, their workers. Since then there has come the recognition, for which credit is largely due to sociologists, that industrial organisations must be treated as functional wholes, and managers themselves have come more and more under scrutiny. One fairly spectacular way of examining managerial behaviour is through management 'games', which in spite of the term are quite a serious business. In essence, these consist of a miniature simulation of an industrial organisation; this may comprise a management team, supplemented in some instances by a small number of operatives who actually produce the 'goods' (e.g. assemblies of bits of cardboard). Such firms may compete against other similarly constituted ones, or play against a 'market' represented by a computer. The people actually filling these roles are usually management trainees, or active managers on refresher courses. From this bald description it is probably difficult to believe that the participants can take the game seriously, or that it can adequately represent the functioning of an industrial organisation. On the first point, it must be realised that participants not only are performing in a manner similar to their tasks in real life but this performance is under public scrutiny from their colleagues; and the fact is that they do become emotionally involved in the game. For instance, in simulated union-management negotiations a considerable amount of mutual antagonism is generated among the managers playing the respective roles. The second objection rests on a misunderstanding of the purpose of simulation: as long as the *processes* going on parallel those in real life, the fact that the situation shows no physical resemblance to an actual industrial organisation is irrelevant. Certainly these studies have thrown a great deal of light on the behaviour of managers, the way in which they reach decisions, interact with their subordinates and the kinds of conflicts in which they become involved. This knowledge, in turn, is helping in the training of a new generation of managers.

While problems of social behaviour in industry receive, for obvious reasons, much attention from psychologists and sociologists, it is doubtful whether they are the most important ones today. Much could be said of the ways in which the study of social behaviour has contributed to our understanding of race prejudice, delinquency and other social evils. But since only one further theme can be discussed, it may be well to select that which is perhaps *the* issue of our day, involving the problem of our continued existence, and that is aggression and conflict.

In spite of prevalent ideas about 'nature red in tooth and claw' there are few, if any, animals which inflict pain, suffering and death on fellow members of their own species in the manner and on the scale this occurs with human beings. Ethologists have described certain control mechanisms in animals, and suggested an explanation why these have become less effective in man:

> The same instinctive inhibition of the fighting drive is found in man. One reason why wholesale slaughter in modern warfare is so relatively easily accomplished is to be found in the modern long-range arms that prevent one witnessing the action of lethal weapons. Our instinctive reluctance to kill is strengthened by the sight of a dying man in a mutilated condition. Hence one is much less reluctant to direct artillery fire at a distant tower, thereby killing the enemy artillery observer, than to cut his throat in a man-to-man fight. Our instinctive disposition has not changed with the development of mechanical long-range killing apparatus. (Tinbergen, *The Study of Instinct*.)

While this may well be one element, it clearly fails to account fully for human cruelty and destructiveness. Hand-to-hand fighting does occur in war, enemies are seen mutilated, and yet the slaughter continues. While it is certain that there is some biological basis of aggression in man, as is argued in somewhat different ways by both Tinbergen and Freud, human behaviour is determined in a far more complex manner. A great deal of study has been devoted to this problem, much of it directed at the childhood origins of aggressive behaviour and the conditions under which it is elicited. Thus it has been demonstrated in a series of experiments, involving, of course, only mild forms of aggression, which show that the presence of another person engaged in aggressive behaviour has the effect of disinhibiting such tendencies in the onlooker; in other words, the behaviour of the 'model' serves to lower such internal barriers as may exist within the onlooker against the outward expression of aggressive tendencies; and if they had not previously been a part of his repertoire, the behaviour witnessed might have taught him and led him to imitate the specific form of aggression. In warfare ample models are available to produce such disinhibition.

It may be noted that the model need not be physically present—film or television will do as well. Such findings have some bearing on a current controversy about the effects of violence shown on these mass media. One school of thought holds that such representations are likely to *reduce* the incidence of actual overt aggression, since they provide a vicarious fantasy outlet. The alternative view is that seeing violence on the screen presents a model for imitation, or has the disinhibiting effect just outlined. A most ingenious test of these rival views was recently undertaken by Peter Schönbach, a psychologist at the University of Frankfurt. His measure of aggression was the severity of punishment thought to be appropriate for a robbery. Taking all the necessary methodological precautions, he arranged to interview on this topic four sets of about one hundred people in the foyers of cinemas:

   I   Before seeing a James Bond film (violent).
   II   Before seeing a Musical (non-violent control film).
   III   After seeing a James Bond film.
   IV   After seeing the Musical.

The crucial measure is the severity of punishment advocated after seeing the James Bond film as compared with the Musical. If the sight of violence offers a fantasy outlet, severity of punishment ought to be less following it; on the other hand, if the second interpretation is valid, people

174

should opt for more harsh punishment after witnessing aggression on the screen. The essential results obtained are given below:

	Percentages of severe punishment advocated	
	Before	*After*
James Bond	28	43
Musical	28	27

This clearly confirms the second interpretation, and thereby strongly reinforces the evidence already accumulated in laboratory experiments.

Turning back to the main issue, man's inhumanity to man, a fundamental contrast with animal fighting lies in the fact that human conflicts take place within a social framework. Sociologists tend to maintain that nowadays war has little, if anything, to do with personal aggressiveness, since it has become institutionalised so that individuals merely play their prescribed roles, however reluctantly, within a scheme of things over which they have no control. Such a view attributes the causation entirely to social influences, apparently minimising the part played by individual motives. Although there is certainly much force in this line of argument, it does perhaps present psychologists with a challenge to discover the conditions under which people give way to social pressures on matters concerning life and death, and perhaps how they can be made more resistant. Recent history is full of instances where people, from generals down to concentration camp guards, pleaded that they were merely 'obeying orders'; most claimed that they disliked what they had to do, and the protestations of some have the ring of truth, although they continued to obey the orders of their superior authorities.

On being reminded of this, most of us take comfort in the thought that this is the kind of thing *they* might do, but *we* never would; can we be really certain? A remarkable study undertaken recently by Milgram[5] offers no ground for complacency. The question he asked was this: supposing a person is ordered by some authority to inflict violence on others: under what conditions will he obey or refuse? The

175

subjects were adult men drawn from a wide range of manual and non-manual occupations. They were placed in a situation whereby they acted as helpers to the experimenter who was allegedly investigating a learning task in another subject (the 'victim'), who was in fact a confederate of the experimenter. The naïve subject was instructed to administer what he believed to be an electric shock of increasing intensity whenever the victim made a mistake. In reality, no shock was received by the supposed victim; but the subject manipulating the shock apparatus, heard responses (actually tape-recorded) that began with mild protests and went up to agonised screams. It was shown that variations in the conditions (e.g. distance from and visibility of victim, presence or absence of experimenter) affected the degree of obedience. All this was overshadowed, however, by the entirely unexpected lack of resistance on the part of the subjects when ordered by an anonymous experimenter to inflict pain on a fellow man. Even when, in order to increase resistance to the commands, subjects were told that the victim had a weak heart, many of them still went on. This does not mean that these people were callous, since they sometimes exhibited agitation and protested to the experimenter, yet stopped short of disobeying the command of authority. From this it has been inferred that it is appallingly easy to order people to do things they would normally be reluctant to do, possibly it suggests a way of inoculating them against such social pressures. Nevertheless, serious ethical problems arise, and some people are strongly of the opinion that such experiments ought not to be undertaken; others feel, like Milgram, that on an issue of such profound importance research is necessary even at the cost of some temporary upset of participants. He did, of course, take great care to inform them fully at the end, and most subjects indicated that they were glad to have taken part.

In any case, this kind of study is rare, though there is another famous one by Sherif[6] from which it emerged that conflict can very readily be fostered between two groups, but the restoration of harmony is much harder. During the last decade interest in the problem of conflict has rapidly grown, and attracted researchers from various disciplines including sociologists, economists, anthropologists, political scientists, historians and others. Much of this effort has concentrated on the discussions and decisions which are a frequent prelude to overt hostilities and, hopefully, a means of avoiding them. Among the many methods used is that of simulation, described earlier in the context of management 'games', and much valuable knowledge about social behaviour in such situations has already accumulated from this joint effort. One final illustration of the potential fruitfulness of such interdisciplinary ventures will be offered. This relates to a study by Holsti,[7] a political scientist, who examined the findings of psychological studies on decision-making under stress. This led him to certain inferences about the characteristics of such decisions in actual political crisis-situations, one of which is as follows: 'decision-makers will perceive their own range of alternatives to be more restricted than those of their adversaries'. He then went back to historical documents relating to the beginning of the First World War and analysed them (taking the necessary precautions to avoid bias) so as to discover whether the political leaders and diplomats at the time did in fact perceive the world in this manner. The result for Great Britain is set out below:

	Choice	Necessity
Self	7	20
Enemies	21	2

The pattern conforms very closely to the predictions: Britain's own freedom of action was seen as greatly restricted, while in complete contrast that of their enemy was regarded as wide open. Now it might be thought doubtful whether the enormous amount of labour invested in this study of decision-makers nearly two generations ago was really worth while. The answer is that it provides strong evidence of the validity of the principles elaborated by psychologists in a variety of apparently 'artificial' experiments. Moreover, if the knowledge thus acquired is passed on to the present generation of decision-makers, they may

stop and take thought when they feel that their opponents
have far more room for manoeuvre than they have themselves: 'Did not those back-room boys tell us that the other
chaps are likely to feel exactly the same? Perhaps we are
both mistaken.' In this manner a potentially catastrophic
deadlock might come to be resolved. Thus apart from its
intrinsic interest, the study of social behaviour may also
have some modest contribution to make towards the easing
of the dangerous tension afflicting the world today.

NOTES

[1] A. Levy-Schoen, *L'image d'autrui chez l'enfant*, Paris: Presses Uni-
versitaires de France, 1964.

[2] J. W. M. Whiting, 'Sorcery, Sin and the Superego', *Nebraska Symposium on Motivation*, 1959.

[3] M. Argyle and J. Dean, 'Eye-contact, distance and affiliation',
Sociometry, 1965, *28*, 289–304.

[4] S. Moscovici and M. Plon, 'Les situations-colloques', *Bulletin de
Psychologie*, 1966, *19*, 702–722.

[5] C. S. Milgram, 'Some conditions of obedience and disobedience to
authority', *Human Relations*, 1965, *18*, 57–76.

[6] M. and C. W. Sherif, *Groups in Harmony and Tension*, New York:
Harper, 1953.

[7] O. R. Holsti, 'Perceptions of time, perceptions of alternatives, and
patterns of communication as factors in crisis decision-making', *Peace
Research Society (International) Papers*, Vol. III, 1965.

Suggested Reading

ZAJONG, ROBERT B., *Social Psychology: an Experimental Approach*,
Belmont (Calif.): Wadsworth, 1966.

EMERSON, A. R., Social Psychology. In D. C. Marsh (ed.): *The Social
Sciences*, London: Routledge & Kegan Paul, 1965.

ARGYLE, M., *The Psychology of Interpersonal Behaviour*, London:
Penguin, 1967.

BEATTIE, J., *Other Cultures*, London: Routledge & Kegan Paul, 1963.

TINBERGEN, N., *Social Behaviour in Animals*, London: Methuen, 1963.

SCHEIN, EDGAR, *Organizational Psychology*, New York: Prentice-Hall,
1965.

BERELSON, BERNARD, *The Behavioral Sciences*, New York: Harper,
1964.

APPENDIX

UNIVERSITIES IN THE UNITED KINGDOM

GUIDE TO ENTRANCE REQUIREMENTS FOR STUDENTS INTENDING TO READ PSYCHOLOGY

*General Requirements for Entrance to
Universities in the United Kingdom*

Most students who are admitted to first degree courses in Universities in England, Wales and Northern Ireland, and a proportion of those admitted to Scottish Universities, have to satisfy the entrance requirements in terms of the General Certificate of Education (G.C.E.). Generally speaking, a certain number of 'O' level and 'A' level passes in prescribed subjects are necessary. There is, however, very much variation in the requirements from one university to another. Full details will be found in the *Compendium of University Entrance Requirements for first degree Courses in UK*, published by the Association of Commonwealth Universities.

Mature students unable to qualify in the manner just described should write directly to the Registrar of the university which they wish to enter. All universities are prepared to consider applications from candidates of this kind, and most universities have special entrance arrangements for them.

The tables which follow are confined to courses leading to Honours degrees. In many universities it is also possible to read Psychology as part of a General Degree in Arts or Science. Most universities offer facilities for post-graduate work in Psychology.

APPENDIX

TABLE I. FACULTIES IN WHICH SINGLE OR DOUBLE OR JOINT
HONOURS COURSES ARE AVAILABLE

University	Faculties in which Honours courses are available			Double or Joint Honours courses
	Arts	Science	Social Studies (or Sciences)	
Aberdeen	√ (M.A.)	√		Psychology and Philosophy or English or Economics
Bangor	√	√		Psychology and Philosophy
Belfast[1]	√	√		Psychology and Philosophy
Birmingham[2]		√		In the Faculty of Arts three-year double Honours courses are available in which Psychology is combined with one of a variety of subjects
Bristol		√	√	In the Faculty of Science, Psychology and Physiology or Zoology, or (in the Faculty of Social Sciences) Psychology and Philosophy or Sociology
Cambridge	Psychology may be taken as Part II of the Natural Sciences Tripos. Undergraduates admitted to it have normally taken Part I in the same Tripos, including Experimental Psychology as a half-subject. In exceptional instances applicants who have taken Part I in the Moral Sciences Tripos are admitted to the Part II course in Psychology			
Cardiff[3] (University College)	√	√	√ B.Sc. (Econ.)	Psychology and Pure Maths or Applied Maths or Physics or Zoology or Philosophy
Dundee			√	Psychology and Statistics or Political Science or Philosophy or Modern Social and Economic History or Geography or Economics or Mathematics

APPENDIX

| University | Faculties in which Honours courses are available | | | Double or Joint Honours courses |
	Arts	Science	Social Studies (or Sciences)	
Durham[4]	√	√	√	Psychology and Philosophy or Economics or Zoology
Edinburgh		√ (B.Sc.)	√ (M.A.)	
Exeter		√	√	Psychology and Math Statistics or Pure Maths or Zoology or Philosophy
Glasgow	√			Psychology and Social Psychology or History of Fine Art or Music or Philosophy or Sociology or Political Economy
Hull		√	√	Psychology and Philosophy or Sociology or Zoology
Keele	All courses lead to Honours in two principal subjects. A B.A. degree is awarded after four years. Psychology is studied in combination with one of a wide range of subjects (e.g. Physics, Politics, Modern Languages)			
Leeds[5]		√		Psychology and Sociology or Statistics or Zoology
Leicester[6]	√	√		
Liverpool	√	√	√	Psychology and Pure Maths
LONDON Bedford College	√	√		Psychology and Philosophy
LONDON Birkbeck College	√	√		Psychology and Philosophy (part-time)
LONDON University College	√	√		Psychology and Philosophy

University	Faculties in which Honours courses are available			Double or Joint Honours courses
	Arts	Science	Social Studies (or Sciences)	
Manchester	√	√		Psychology and Mathematics or Physics or Pharmacology or Physiology or Zoology
Newcastle upon Tyne[7]				Psychology and Philosophy
Nottingham	√	√	√	Psychology and Physiology or Philosophy or Mathematics or Zoology
Oxford	√			Psychology and Philosophy or Physiology
Reading	√	√		Psychology and Economics
Sheffield	√	√	√	Psychology and Philosophy or Sociology
Southampton		√	√	Psychology and Sociology or Statistics
St. Andrews	See Note 8 below			
Stirling	Honours Courses in Psychology are under consideration			
Strathclyde[9]	√			
Sussex	The university is organised in Schools in which undergraduates specialise in some particular discipline. Psychology may be taken as a main subject in the School of Biological Sciences, the School of Educational Studies or the School of Social Studies			Experimental Psychology and Mathematics
Swansea[10]	√	√	√	

APPENDIX

NOTES

[1] At Belfast a post-graduate degree of **B.Ed.** (Psychology) is awarded to graduates in any subject, after a two-year course of study.

[2] The Department at the University of Birmingham came into existence in October 1965. It is located in the Faculty of Science and Engineering. Apart from preparing students for the degree of B.Sc. in this Faculty, students in the Faculty of Arts and in the Faculty of Commerce and Social Science will also be prepared in psychology as part of Joint Honours degrees.

[3] At Cardiff the B.Sc. (Econ.) is regarded as equivalent to a Joint Honours degree with Psychology as one subject. The length of the course is four years if the student has only passed in two subjects at A-level, and three years if he has passed in three subjects.

[4] At Durham, a student can take Psychology in preparing for the degree of M.Ed. This degree is open to those with a qualification to teach.

[5] At Leeds, the combined Honours course in Psychology and Sociology leads to a B.A. (Combined Studies) degree. The courses in which Psychology is combined with Statistics *or* Zoology lead to B.Sc. (Combined Studies) degree.

[6] At Leicester there are B.A. and B.Sc. Combined Studies degrees but no Joint Honours courses. Students who read Psychology as their main, three-year subject in a Combined Studies degree are deemed to have an Honours degree in Psychology for many post-graduate purposes.

[7] At Newcastle upon Tyne it is expected that an Honours course in Psychology will be introduced in 1967/8 in both the Faculty of Arts and the Faculty of Science.

[8] (a) St. Andrews University, which at present (1966) comprises Queen's College, Dundee, and St. Salvator's and St. Mary's Colleges in St. Andrews, will become two universities as from 1 August 1967, namely (1) the University of Dundee and (2) the University of St. Andrews.

(b) Until 1961 there was a flourishing Honours school in Psychology at St. Andrews, in which Honours Psychology was taken in conjunction with Logic and Metaphysics *or* Moral Philosophy *or* Political Economy but since then only a severely restricted first year class has been available for Arts and Science students.

(c) It is now recommended (May 1966) that there be a graduating course in Psychology in the new University of St. Andrews.

[9] At Strathclyde a Joint Honours course in Psychology and Mathematics is planned for 1967/8.

[10] At Swansea, students preparing for the degree of B.Sc. (Econ.) can combine Psychology with one or two of the following subjects: Anthropology, Economics, Geography, Philosophy, Politics, Social Administration, Sociology or Statistics.

TABLE II. ENTRANCE REQUIREMENTS FOR SINGLE OR DOUBLE HONOURS COURSES IN PSYCHOLOGY

University	Degree	Length of course (years)	A-level passes	Named O-level passes
Aberdeen	M.A.	4	2	
	B.Sc.	4	2	
Bangor	B.A. } B.Sc. }	3	3	Mathematics
Belfast	B.A.	3/4	2	
	B.Sc.	3/4	2	Mathematics, Physics, Chemistry, and French or German or Russian
Birmingham	B.Sc.	3	3	Mathematics
Bristol	B.Sc. Faculty of Science	3	2 (Science)	Mathematics
	B.Sc. Faculty of Social Science	3	2*	
Cambridge	The basic entrance requirements for taking the Natural Sciences Tripos are handled by the Colleges. Part I is a two-year course in which candidates take three to four subjects (or combinations of subjects and half-subjects), while Part II is normally a one-year course in a single subject			
Cardiff	B.Sc.	3	2:3†	
	B.A. } B.Sc. } (Econ.) }	3	2	Mathematics

* Two A-level passes in an approved subject which means a subject in the examination of the General Certificate of Education which is included in the approved list of subjects for the purposes of eligibility for matriculation.

† A student with only two passes at A-level must spend four years in preparing for a science degree. With three passes, three years suffice.

University	Degree	Length of course (years)	A-level passes	Named O-level passes
Dundee	M.A. Joint Honours	4	2/3	The Certificate of Attestation of the Scottish Universities Central Board is required
Durham	B.Sc.	3	2 or 3	
	B.A.	3	2	
Edinburgh	M.A.	4	2 or 3	
	B.Sc.	4	2 or 3	Mathematics
Exeter	B.Sc.	3	2	Mathematics
	B.A.	3	2	
Glasgow	M.A.	4	3	
Hull	B.A. } B.Sc. }	3	3	
Keele	B.A.	4	2	
Leeds	B.Sc.	4	2	Mathematics
Leicester	B.A. } B.Sc. }	3	3	
Liverpool	B.A.	3	2 or 3	Latin or Greek or Mathematics
	B.Sc.	3 or 4	2 or 3	Zoology or Biology
LONDON Bedford College	B.A.	3	2	Foreign Language Mathematics is desirable
	B.Sc.	3	2	Mathematics is desirable

University	Degree	Length of course (years)	A-level passes	Named O-level passes
LONDON Birkbeck College	B.A.	4 (part time) 3 (full time)	2	Mathematics
	B.Sc.	4 (part time) 3 (full time)	2	
LONDON University College	B.A.	3	2	
	B.Sc.	3	2	
Manchester	B.A.	3	3	Mathematics and a Science subject
	B.Sc.	3	3	Mathematics
Newcastle	It is intended to establish a single Honours course in Psychology in 1967 or 1968			
Nottingham	B.A.	3	2	Mathematics
	B.Sc.	3	3 in Science	
Oxford	At present there are only joint Honours courses. Single Honours courses are under consideration			
Reading	B.A.	3	2	Mathematics
	B.Sc.	3	3	Mathematics
Sheffield	B.A.	3	2 or 3	
	B.Sc.	3	3 in Science	
Southampton	B.Sc.	3	3, including at least 2 in Science	
	B.Sc. (Soc.Sci.)	3	2	

University	Degree	Length of course (years)	A-level passes	Named O-level passes
St. Andrews	See Note 8, Table 1.			
Stirling	See Table 1.			
Strathclyde	B.A.	4	2	Mathematics and one Foreign Language
Sussex	B.Sc.	3	2, normally in Science	
	B.A.	3	2	
Swansea	B.A. } B.Sc. }	3	3	Mathematics

Note: Where '3' is stated as the number of A-level passes required this is not to be taken rigidly. Some universities (e.g. Leicester) are content, in exceptional circumstances, with a pass in two subjects.

APPENDIX

A. PSYCHOLOGY AND ECONOMICS

University	Degree	Length of course (years)	A-level passes
Aberdeen	M.A.	4	2
Birmingham*	B.Soc.Sc.	3	3
Dundee (from 1 August 1967)	M.A.	4	2/3 The Certificate of Attestation of the Scottish Universities Entrance Board is required
Durham	B.A.	3	2
Glasgow	M.A.	4	3 including one Foreign Language
Keele	B.A.	4	2
Reading*	B.A.	3	2
Swansea	B.Sc. (Econ.)	3	3

* A pass in Mathematics is required at O-level.

APPENDIX

B. PSYCHOLOGY AND MATHEMATICS (OR MATHEMATICAL STATISTICS)

University	Degree	Length of course (years)	A-level passes
Birmingham	B.A.	3	3 including Pure or Applied or Pure and Applied Mathematics
Cardiff	B.Sc.	3	3 including Pure Maths or high mark in Pure and Applied Mathematics
Dundee (from 1 August 1967)	M.A. (Statistics)	4	2/3 The Certificate of Attestation of the Scottish Universities Entrance Board is required
Exeter*	B.Sc.	3	2 or 3
Keele	B.A.	4	2
Leeds	B.Sc.	3	3
Liverpool	B.A.	3	2 or 3 Pure and Applied Maths, or Pure Maths or Maths (with Statistics and Physics)

* Exeter offers a combined Honours degree either in 'Psychology and Pure Mathematics' or in 'Psychology and Mathematical Statistics'.

University	Degree	Length of course (years)	A-level passes
Manchester†	B.Sc.	3	3 including Mathematics
Nottingham†	B.Sc.	3	3 including Mathematics
Sheffield*	B.A.	3	2/3 including Pure Mathematics
Southampton	B.Sc. (Soc.Sci.)	3	2
Strathclyde	B.A.	4	2 including Mathematics
Sussex	B.Sc.	3	2 normally in Science
Swansea	B.Sc. (Econ.)	3	3 including Mathematics

† Candidates must be accepted by both the Department of Mathematics and the Department of Psychology, and graduate in Psychology. Normally they take Psychology as one of three subjects in their first year, but in special circumstances may transfer from Honours Mathematics to joint Psychology–Mathematics at the end of their first year. Nottingham differs from Manchester in not allowing transfers after the first year.

* The title of the degree is 'Psychology, Mathematics and Statistics'.

Note: (i) At Leeds, the Combined Studies degrees normally require a four-year course. Exemption from the first year of this course is invariably required and depends on A-level performance. Three A-level passes are required if Mathematics is taken as a single subject, otherwise two A-level passes suffice. A pass in Physics at O-level is required. (ii) At Southampton, the emphasis is on the use of statistical techniques rather than on their mathematical derivation.

C. PSYCHOLOGY AND PHILOSOPHY

University	Degree	Length of course (years)	A-level passes
Aberdeen	M.A.	4	2
Bangor	B.A. ⎱ B.Sc. ⎰	3	3
Belfast	B.A.	3/4	2
Birmingham	B.A.	3	3
Bristol	B.Sc.	3	2
Cardiff	B.A.	3	2
Dundee (from 1 August 1967)	M.A.	4	2/3 The Certificate of Attestation of the Scottish Universities Central Board is required
Durham	B.A.	3	2
Exeter	B.A.	3	2
Glasgow	M.A.	4	3
Hull	B.A.	3	3
Keele	B.A.	4	2
LONDON Bedford College	B.A.	3	2

University	Degree	Length of course (years)	A-level passes
LONDON Birkbeck College	B.A.	4 (part time)	2
LONDON University College	B.A.	3	2
Newcastle	B.A.	3	2
Nottingham	B.A.	3	2
Sheffield*	B.A.	3	2/3
Swansea	B.Sc. (Econ.)	3	3

* The B.A. is given when the joint degree is awarded in the Faculty of Arts, and the B.A. (Econ.) when it is awarded in the Faculty of Economics and Social Studies.

Note: At Birmingham, Bristol, Durham, Exeter, Nottingham, Sheffield, Wales, a pass in Mathematics is a specified O-level requirement. At Durham and Exeter Latin or Greek is named as an alternative. London University requires two foreign languages, including one Classical, at O-level. At Oxford there are no formal requirements, but Biology is useful.

D. PSYCHOLOGY AND SOCIOLOGY

University	Degree	Length of course (years)	A-level passes
Birmingham	B.A.	3	3
	B.Soc.Sc.	3	3
Bristol*	B.Sc. (Soc.Sci.)	3	2
Glasgow	M.A.	4	3
Hull	B.A.	3	3
Keele	B.A.	4	2
Leeds	B.A.	3	2 Mathematics and History
Liverpool	B.A. (Social Studies)	3	2 or 3
Sheffield	B.A.	3	2/3
Southampton	B.Sc. (Soc.Sci.)	3	2
Swansea	B.Sc. (Econ.)	3	3

Note: At Birmingham, Leeds and Sheffield a pass in Mathematics at O-level is required.

* At Bristol O-level Mathematics is required.

E. PSYCHOLOGY AND ZOOLOGY

University	Degree	Length of course (years)	A-level passes
Bristol*	B.Sc.	3	2
Cardiff	B.Sc.	3:4	3:2
Durham†	B.Sc.	3	2/3
Exeter†	B.Sc.	3	2
Hull	B.Sc.	3	3
Keele‡	B.A.	4	2
Leeds†	B.Sc.	3	2/3
Manchester†	B.Sc.	3	3
Nottingham†	B.Sc.	3	3

* At Bristol O-level Mathematics is required.
† At Durham, Exeter, Leeds, Manchester and Nottingham a pass in Mathematics at O-level is required.
‡ At Keele it is Biology (not Zoology) which is combined with Psychology.

F. PSYCHOLOGY AND SOCIAL PSYCHOLOGY

University	Degree	Length of course (years)	A-level passes
Glasgow	M.A.	4	3

G. PSYCHOLOGY AND PHYSIOLOGY

University	Degree	Length of course (years)	A-level passes
Bristol*	B.Sc.	3	3
Cambridge	B.A.	This is Part II of the Tripos and is a one-year course. A good Class I or II(i) in Part I is normally required. Candidates should have taken Physiology and Experimental Psychology in Part I	
Manchester	B.Sc.	3	3 Preferably including Chemistry
Oxford	B.A.	3	No formal requirements but Physics and Chemistry very desirable

* At Bristol O-level Mathematics is required, and A-level Chemistry is desirable.

H. PSYCHOLOGY AND PHARMACOLOGY

University	Degree	Length of course (years)	A-level passes
Manchester	B.Sc.	3	3

I. PSYCHOLOGY AND PHYSICS

University	Degree	Length of course (years)	A-level passes
Manchester*	B.Sc.	3	3

* Candidates must be accepted by both the Department of Physics and the Department of Psychology, and graduate in Psychology. Their first year is devoted to Physics and Mathematics, and the second and third years divided evenly between Physics (and Electronics) and Psychology.

Note: At the University of Dundee it is expected that Double Honours courses in Psychology and Political Science *or* Modern Social and Economic History will continue, in the Faculty of Social Sciences.

Author Index

Subject Index